Which Road Ahead –
Government or Market?

Which Road Ahead – Government or Market?

OLIVER KNIPPING AND RICHARD WELLINGS

The Institute of Economic Affairs

First published in Great Britain in 2012 by
The Institute of Economic Affairs
2 Lord North Street
Westminster
London sw1p 3lb
in association with Profile Books Ltd

The mission of the Institute of Economic Affairs is to improve public understanding of the fundamental institutions of a free society, with particular reference to the role of markets in solving economic and social problems.

A CIP catalogue record for this book is available from the British Library.

ISBN 978 0 255 36619 9
eISBN 978 0 255 36679 3

Many IEA publications are translated into languages other than English or are reprinted. Permission to translate or to reprint should be sought from the Director General at the address above.

Typeset in Stone by MacGuru Ltd
info@macguru.org.uk

Printed and bound in Britain by Hobbs the Printers

CONTENTS

THE AUTHORS

Dr Oliver Knipping is president of the Institute for Free Enterprise, a German free-market think tank. Prior to receiving a PhD from University College London (2002) he graduated from Humboldt University Berlin in economics (1998). He is vice-president in a global telecommunications company.

Dr Richard Wellings is deputy editorial director at the Institute of Economic Affairs and director of the IEA's transport unit. He was educated at Oxford and the London School of Economics, where he completed a PhD on transport policy in 2004. Richard is the author or editor of several papers, books and reports, including *Towards Better Transport* (Policy Exchange, 2008) and *A Beginner's Guide to Liberty* (Adam Smith Institute, 2009). He is a Senior Fellow of the Cobden Centre and the Economic Policy Centre.

FOREWORD

One of the great achievements of the 1980s and 1990s was the privatisation of nationalised utilities. It should be said that these privatisations were not wholly successful. In many cases, the businesses concerned became more and more heavily regulated, and the issue of corporate structure was not always dealt with imaginatively. Nevertheless, in the various privatised utilities, there has been some mix of lower prices, greater innovation and greater investment to an extent that was certainly not envisaged by the opponents of privatisation at the time.

There is very little discussion, however, about the privatisation of the road network – another utility, just like the railways, airports and energy industries. This is perhaps surprising. Much of the road network was once private; there are many networks of private roads elsewhere in the world; there are many different types of road and it is hardly likely that government ownership will be appropriate for all these types; and there is no natural monopoly.

At first it might be thought that roads are, indeed, a natural monopoly. After all, there is only one M40 that can be used by cars and buses from London to Birmingham. There are, however, many different ways to travel from London to Birmingham – including at least three major road routes and at least two different train companies. There is the potential for intense competition between different modes of travel between any two destinations. Furthermore, there are alternatives to travelling – at least for business meetings – such as video-conferencing. In any case, economists would not normally suggest that nationalisation is the correct response to the existence of natural monopolies. Normally the policy approach to be adopted in the case of natural monopolies would be the regulation of a private monopoly – though the authors of this monograph explicitly reject such regulation as unnecessary and undesirable.

It is also worth noting that there would seem to be widespread dissatisfaction with roads in their current state under current ownership. There is chronic congestion in many areas; many minor roads are in a very poor state of repair; and road projects are regularly rejected by government that would bring a very high ratio of benefits to costs.

It is against this background that Oliver Knipping and Richard Wellings show how the road network can be privatised. The authors counter many of the conventional arguments against privatisation while explaining carefully the benefits of privatisation. The authors are very aware of the different problems that might arise from the privatisation of different types of road (from motorways to residential cul-de-sacs) and propose approaches to privatisation that are appropriate in each case. The authors do not neglect, of course, the relationship between the privatisation and the reform of road taxation.

With private ownership of roads would come private management. There would be incentives to maintain roads, find ways of reducing congestion and price roads in a way that maximised their use. Although there have been many criticisms of the way in which railways were privatised, one of the benefits has been that professional marketing, management and pricing have led to an explosion in usage. The same could happen with the road network. Local communities could look after and control access to the most minor roads, though it is more likely that large firms would own and manage motorways, making the best use of technology and pricing to promote free-flowing traffic and high standards of safety.

As the authors note, planning restrictions would also have to be liberalised in order to get the best out of road privatisation – especially in terms of reducing monopoly power, but also to ensure that schemes were developed that reduced congestion bottlenecks.

Overall, this study is a holistic and wide-ranging examination of the prospects for road privatisation and related issues. It provides excellent material for policy makers, academics and students of transport and logistics. The IEA recommends this monograph as an important contribution to the debate about road privatisation.

PHILIP BOOTH

Editorial and Programme Director,
Institute of Economic Affairs
Professor of Insurance and Risk Management,
Cass Business School, City University
July 2012

The views expressed in this Hobart Paper are, as in all IEA publications, those of the authors and not those of the Institute (which has no corporate view), its managing trustees, Academic Advisory Council Members or senior staff.

ACKNOWLEDGEMENTS

This publication has been made possible by the support of the Nigel Vinson Charitable Foundation. The directors and trustees of the IEA thank the Rt Hon. Lord Vinson of Roddam Dene, LVO, for both his intellectual and financial input.

SUMMARY

- Government ownership and management of roads
  is inefficient and ensures that the transport system is
  unresponsive to consumer demand.
- It has been estimated, for example, that congestion imposes
  costs of £20 billion per year in the UK, over £90 billion in the
  European Union as a whole and £75 billion in the USA.
- Construction of new roads in the UK has collapsed in recent
  years. The average benefit–cost ratio of cancelled projects
  is 3.2 and the average benefit–cost ratio of projects that are
  deferred is 6.8. Meanwhile, local public transport projects
  are regularly funded despite average benefit–cost ratios of
  1.8. Government control leads poor-value projects to be
  undertaken for political reasons and good-value projects to be
  rejected.
- The UK has about half as much motorway per vehicle
  kilometre travelled as other major EU countries. Many
  of those other EU countries have considerable private
  management, finance or ownership of the motorway network.
- The management of local roads is no better than the
  management of major roads. There are 1.5 million potholes
  on the road network and 40 per cent of road users believe
  that road surfaces have got much worse over the last decade.
  Drivers spend hundreds of millions of pounds on repairs to
  vehicles resulting from pothole damage but local authority

spending on filling potholes in 2010/11 was only £90 million.

- Government and local authorities have weak incentives to determine and allocate road maintenance budgets more effectively as they are not directly charging motorists for using roads and gain little from improving the quality of service to drivers. Feedback mechanisms between voters and local councils and national government are very poor, with infrequent elections being dominated by other issues.
- Many of the traditional arguments against private ownership of roads are not valid. Roads are not natural monopolies, although market power will be encouraged through rigid planning controls. Also, local roads are club goods rather than public goods. Private road owners would also have much stronger incentives to integrate roads with other parts of the transport system than currently exist.
- Motorways and major roads should be privatised. This could raise about £150 billion in the UK. Owners would be able to determine charges for road use. Vehicle Excise Duty should be abolished and fuel duty reduced by at least 75 per cent. Owners would be free to introduce innovative systems of regulation and traffic management.
- Different approaches should be used for minor roads. Local roads should be owned and managed by local residents and businesses. This has happened via private road associations in Sweden, where road management costs have been reduced but the quality of services provided is high.
- The benefits from privatisation will be reduced if the government tries to regulate a private road network. On the other hand, the benefits from road privatisation will be enhanced if the government simultaneously reforms policies on land-use planning and public transport.

TABLES, FIGURES AND BOXES

1 INTRODUCTION

Adam Smith wrote that good roads are 'the greatest of all improvements ... [they] put the remote parts of the country more nearly upon a level with those in the neighbourhood of the town' (Smith, 1776: I. 11. 14). But Smith also viewed roads as public works to be provided, managed and owned by government.[1] Smith was right about the economic importance of roads, but, we believe, wrong on the issue of ownership.

Across the world, state-owned roads are characterised by endemic congestion, high accident rates, poor maintenance and wasteful investment. While government roads have undoubtedly brought benefits such as reduced travel times, lower trade costs, economies of scale and so on, a strong case can be made that the benefits would have been far greater had they been built and managed by the private sector. Indeed, both empirical evidence and economic theory support the contention that private ownership would bring significant efficiency gains and deliver infrastructure that was far better suited to the preferences of road users.

Current systems of government control are highly inefficient and unresponsive to consumer demand. It has been estimated, for example, that congestion imposes costs of £20 billion per year in

---

1   See Smith (1776: V. 1. 69–89). Importantly, Smith argued that roads were better managed by local and provincial institutions rather than national treasuries.

the UK (Blythe, 2005), over €120 billion in the European Union as a whole (EC, 2003: 37) and $115 billion in the United States (Shrank et al., 2010). In 2010, more than two thousand people were killed in road accidents in the UK and 25,000 seriously injured (DfT, 2011a), while around 35,000 people died on roads in the European Union (EU, 2010) and a further 35,000 in the USA (NHTSA, 2011).

Government roads also impose significant costs on taxpayers to fund both new construction and maintenance. The British government spent £9.5 billion in 2010 (DfT, 2011b).[2] These large sums of money are not spent efficiently. Investment has tended to be directed according to political priorities rather than according to consumer demand.[3]

Figure 1 compares the construction of new motorways and trunk roads with growth in traffic over the last quarter of a century. Traffic levels – and indeed congestion – increased substantially until the onset of recession, and are forecast to rise by over a third from current levels by 2035 (ibid.). By contrast, the construction of new road capacity has collapsed – suggesting supply has become almost completely divorced from demand. This reflects the nature of state road ownership, where the supply of new capacity is decided by politicians and bureaucrats. The collapse in new road construction since the 1980s resulted from a deliberate government policy to focus investment on public transport, and railways in particular, rather than roads (DETR, 1998).

Figure 2 shows that, adjusted for traffic levels, Britain has a

---

2   Figure includes spending by both the Highways Agency and local authorities, most on maintenance (see DfT, 2011b).

3   There are, of course, elaborate appraisal systems which seek to prioritise investment according to explicit criteria. Nevertheless, there remains a strong element of political control, for example over funding of new road schemes.

Figure 1   **Motorway and trunk road completions (lane km) and road traffic (billion vehicle km), 1985–2010***

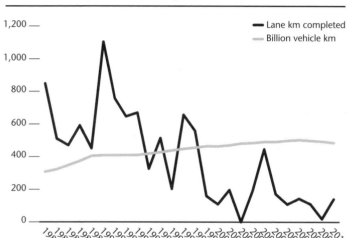

*Motorway and trunk road completions for England; traffic statistics for Great Britain.
Source: *Transport Statistics Great Britain*, 1986–2011 editions.

far smaller motorway network than most other major economies. Moreover, together with the Netherlands, it has the worst levels of inter-urban congestion in western Europe (Schade et al., 2006: 10). International comparisons reveal huge variations in policy between state-owned road networks. The UK's long-standing 'anti-roads' approach[4] contrasts markedly with policy in China, where approximately two thousand miles of motorway have been constructed every year since the late 1990s. But a significant part of this new network has been constructed in outlying regions for

4   This approach dates back at least until the 1920s, when the Ministry of Transport prevented entrepreneurs from building a privately financed motorway network (Plowden, 1971).

Figure 2 **Motorway length (km) per billion vehicle km***

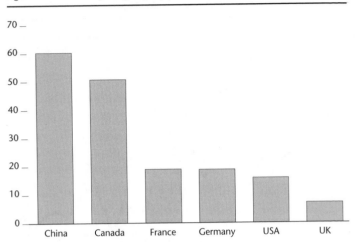

*Data from latest available year.
Sources: International Road Federation (2011), DfT (2011b) and authors' estimates.

political reasons and carries little traffic. Inefficient investment is a pervasive aspect of state ownership at a variety of geographical scales. Resources have been wasted providing overcapacity in many areas while other locations suffer from severe overcrowding.

Despite the deployment of cost–benefit analysis, there is strong evidence that the British government favours capital spending on public transport over roads, despite much lower estimated returns. Furthermore, the most valuable road schemes are not necessarily pursued. As a result of the Comprehensive Spending Review in autumn 2010, several strategic road schemes have been deferred, cancelled or placed under review. As shown in Table 1, even the cancelled schemes have a benefit–cost ratio almost three times higher than High Speed 2, which has been authorised by the government and forms the core of its long-term rail investment policy. Similarly, *The Eddington Transport Study* (2006) found that road schemes had far higher estimated economic returns than public transport projects, yet government transport policy has continued to prioritise the latter.

Table 1 **Benefit–cost ratios of transport projects**

		Benefit–cost ratio
Strategic road schemes (post-2010 review)	Average for those cancelled	3.2
	Average for those under review	4.2
	Average for those deferred	6.8
High Speed 2 (London to West Midlands)		1.2
Eddington Report survey	Strategic roads	4.7
	Local roads	4.2
	Rail	2.8
	Local public transport	1.8

Sources: Eddington (2006); Dodgson (2009); DfT (2012b); Odell (2012)

Such resource allocation problems apply to government road management as well as new construction. As a result large sections of state-owned networks are in a poor state of repair, imposing significant costs on road users, in terms of poorer safety, slower speeds and damage to vehicles. Box 1 examines particular problems associated with road maintenance by local governments in the UK.

The resulting economic cost goes beyond congestion and

Box 1 **Government neglect of road maintenance**
The large number of potholes on Britain's roads is one of
the most obvious manifestations of government failure – a
classic example of resource misallocation by the state. The
Automobile Association (AA) estimates that there are 1.5
million potholes on the road network, defined in their surveys
as holes over six inches in diameter and two inches deep
(AA, 2011: 2). A 2008 survey revealed that 64 per cent of AA
members thought that the condition of road surfaces had
deteriorated over the previous ten years, with 40 per cent
believing road surfaces had got 'much worse'.*

Local councils spent £35 million in 2010/11 compensating
drivers for damage to vehicles caused by potholes (AIA,
2012). These compensation payments represent just a tiny
fraction of the costs faced by motorists. In general, councils
are liable for damages only if the pothole has already been
reported. Moreover, many motorists choose not to seek
redress owing to the transaction costs involved or because
they are not aware that they can do so. Also, much of the
damage from potholes is gradual in nature and cannot
be ascribed to a single incident, even though it leads to
significantly higher vehicle maintenance costs, particularly
for suspension systems, wheels and tyres. Estimates of the
annual cost of these repairs vary enormously, from hundreds
of millions of pounds to several billion.† By contrast, local

---

taxpayer subsidies. Suboptimal road networks have other
profound economic implications. If transport costs are artificially
raised by congestion, poor maintenance or the prohibition of
new road capacity, the costs of exchange are also increased. The

authority spending on filling potholes in 2010/11 was £90 million (ibid.). This form of maintenance is also inefficient, since emergency patch-and-mend programmes are more expensive than systematic resurfacing (ibid.).

Unfortunately local authorities have weak incentives to determine and allocate road maintenance budgets more effectively. Since councils are not directly charging motorists for using their roads, they gain little from improving the quality of service to drivers. Moreover, transaction costs enable them to offload most of the costs of poor maintenance on to vehicle owners. The feedback mechanisms between voters and local councils are very poor with infrequent elections being dominated by other issues. By contrast, private road owners would have strong commercial incentives to adopt efficient maintenance schedules and provide road surfaces of a standard expected by their customers. In the case of private roads owned and managed by local residents and businesses one could also expect substantial benefits from local knowledge and the resulting ability to report and repair faults quickly (see Box 5).

* 'Snow and ice cause 40% increase in road damage', AA, 16 February 2009, http://www.theaa.com/public_affairs/news/pothole-problem-follows-severe-weather.html
† See, for example, http://www.potholes.co.uk/facts

division of labour, competition, economies of scale and associated productivity gains are hampered. The pattern of economic activity is compressed into smaller, more localised markets. Conversely, if governments subsidise road schemes that would not be commercially viable, the spatial pattern of economic activity may be artificially extended, unfairly favouring large companies and creating diseconomies of scale (Carson, 2008). The negative economic impact of the tax increases needed to fund such infrastructure should of course also be considered (see Minford and Wang, 2011).

As well as distorting patterns of trade, state ownership hampers innovation. The continual problem-solving, experimentation and discovery that characterise entrepreneurial free markets are stifled by government control (Kirzner, 1997). The effects are uncertain and impossible to quantify since one cannot know what innovations road entrepreneurs would have produced under a free-market system. Nevertheless, the chapters that follow explore options open to private road owners for improving the productivity of road infrastructure, including the application of new technology, a more flexible approach to regulations and so on.

A further objection to state ownership is that roads are thereby subject to what might be termed the 'tragedy of the commons'. Governments effectively prevent individuals and community groups from managing access to and use of infrastructure. Public roads have therefore become arenas for crime and antisocial behaviour. Indeed, across the world entrepreneurs and communities have responded by creating private streets where residents and businesses feel safer (Roth, 2006; Beito et al., 2004).

Although in modern times private ownership has been relatively limited in scope, there are enough case studies to support the contention that privatisation would bring significant benefits. While governments have severely constrained the property rights of road owners, it would appear that private infrastructure has generally exhibited lower levels of congestion, fewer accidents and less crime. A number of examples are described in Chapter 3. But it is important to acknowledge that the full benefits of private ownership will arise only when the role of government is greatly diminished – in other words when private owners are free to negotiate routes,[5] set toll rates, control access and determine rules for users. The absence of such property rights limits the availability of empirical evidence relevant to the debate. In many instances, state intervention is so pervasive that private ownership is largely nominal. The outcomes thus provide only limited evidence for the benefits of genuine private ownership. Similarly, the problems experienced in 'sham privatisations', such as public–private partnerships, where high levels of state control are retained and minimal risk accepted by the private sector (see Parker, 2009a), are of little importance to the debate.

The limited availability of relevant empirical evidence means that the case for privatisation must partly rely on the lessons of economic theory. In particular, Austrian economics and public choice theory provide incisive critiques of state ownership based on the inability of government actors to access and use information and engage in entrepreneurial activity, and the impact of government ownership on incentive structures.

Central planning and economic calculation

Governments provide roads using central planning methods similar in many ways to those used in the Soviet Union (Roth,

---

5   Issues relating to holdouts, compulsory purchase and eminent domain are discussed in Chapter 3.

1996: 1).[6] But central planners are unable to allocate resources efficiently because they cannot access the dispersed and *subjective*, time- and place-specific knowledge held by individuals (Hayek, 1945). By contrast, entrepreneurs in free markets are able to tap this knowledge via the price mechanism, which transmits information about changing individual preferences to market participants. In a roads system under government control, relevant market prices may be absent, making it impossible to calculate accurately costs and outputs (see Mises, 1949: 696).[7] Even if some prices are available, these are likely to be distorted by interventions such as taxes and regulations, which make it more difficult for officials to allocate resources efficiently. Compared with private enterprise, state-owned activities are therefore limited in their ability to respond to changes in supply and demand and to discover new profit opportunities.

Private entrepreneurs have strong incentives to engage in this dynamic market discovery process that experiments and innovates in order to solve problems and satisfy consumer wants. As business owners, they have a strong financial incentive to make the most of profit opportunities. By contrast, government officials lack this 'commercial mindedness' (Mises, 1935) and their financial rewards and status will typically be largely unrelated to exploiting new business opportunities. Indeed, within state bureaucracies there will be significant downsides associated with taking entrepreneurial risks.

6　The planning process may take place at national, regional or local level, or some combination of the above. Cost–benefit analyses may be deployed or there may be some element of competition. Free-market processes such as entrepreneurial discovery are, however, typically absent.

7　These arguments also apply to the calculation of 'social' costs (see Cordato, 2004).

Government failure

The incentive structures under state ownership mean that roads policy is likely to be driven by political incentives rather than the entrepreneurial discovery and satisfaction of consumer preferences. Politicians may direct road investment in order to raise their chance of getting re-elected (see Downs, 1957). Alternatively, new infrastructure might be provided for a politician's local area as part of the bargaining process over government spending decisions (see Buchanan and Tullock, 1962). The political process is also subject to influence by special interest groups, which have far stronger incentives to engage in lobbying than dispersed groups such as taxpayers and motorists (Olson, 1965) . To some extent, roads policy may be captured by powerful corporate interests seeking to shut out competition by the creation of unfair privileges (see Stigler, 1971). Alternatively policy may be unduly influenced by bureaucrats seeking to increase their status or maximise their budgets (Niskanen, 1971; Dunleavy, 1991). A further explanation is that officials may develop an irrational attachment to particular schemes which, for reasons of professional achievement, they wish to see implemented before retiring. While the relative impact of these different incentives varies, the overall effect is that the allocation of resources is largely based on arbitrary political and bureaucratic decisions rather than on market processes. We have already noted how highly profitable road schemes are not undertaken. At the same time, unprofitable schemes are followed through for political reasons – not just in public transport. In combination with the economic calculation problems described above, the incentives facing politicians and bureaucrats have resulted in a high degree of 'government failure' on state-owned roads. The specific impact of these factors in one well-known case is discussed in Box 2.

Box 2 **The 'Bridge to Nowhere'**

The Humber Bridge illustrates well the shortcomings of government road schemes. The project, completed in 1981, links the north bank of the River Humber, seven miles from the city of Hull in East Yorkshire, to sparsely populated Lincolnshire across the river. Previously the journey involved a long diversion around the end of the estuary or an inconvenient ferry trip.*

The scheme was politically inspired from the start. Its biggest supporter was Hull Corporation (the local authority), which believed there would be substantial economic benefits from expanding the city's hinterland. Barbara Castle, Minister of Transport, pledged that the Labour government would fund the bridge during the 1966 Hull North by-election campaign. This was widely interpreted as a blatant bribe to voters (Brittan, 2012). Labour won the crucial by-election and the subsequent general election two months later. The 1960s were also the heyday of regional planning and the government saw the bridge as a key element of a new 'Maritime Industrial Development Area' (Simon, 1984).

Well before the bridge opened the failures of central planning were all too apparent. Construction costs had overrun by approximately 50 per cent in real terms. Worse still, traffic was only one sixth of the level projected. Regional policy goals had also proved unrealistic. The region was undergoing rapid industrial decline and the population was stagnating. Transport planners had also blundered by failing to make the bridge a major part of the strategic network. Two lightly used motorways had been built in parallel on either side of the estuary when the bridge would have enabled one to suffice (ibid.). On the other hand, there was no proper road network south of the bridge.

The scheme had largely been financed via a loan from central government to the Humber Bridge Board. Although toll revenues covered operating costs, the above factors meant the loan could never be paid off. In 2008, local newspapers launched a campaign to abolish the tolls, supported by MPs and councillors. In 2011 the Chancellor of the Exchequer agreed to write off £150 million of the debt, allowing toll rates to be halved.[†]

The Humber Bridge may be contrasted with the development of privately owned roads in several ways. Firstly, politics drove the project rather than economic calculation. Secondly, in the absence of price signals its planners badly miscalculated consumer demand. Thirdly, like many big government projects that offload financial risks on to taxpayers, the scheme was 'gold-plated' in the absence of normal commercial incentives to economise. It produced the longest single-span suspension bridge in the world when cheaper options were available. Finally, the incoherence of charging for the use of the bridge while not charging for competing roads and also not adequately developing the related road network means that what was once the longest single-span bridge in the world is rather like a minor local road between villages.

* The ferry trip did at least start in the centre of Hull, rather than seven miles from Hull, however.
† 'Humber Bridge tolls to be halved, Chancellor confirms', *Hull Daily Mail*, 29 November 2011.

Road pricing

It might be contended, however, that many of the problems observed result from the absence of pricing on most roads, rather than government ownership per se. There is some merit in this argument, particularly with regard to congestion.

Without pricing, journey costs do not reflect the scarcity of road space at particular locations at particular times. Motorists do not pay the full marginal costs they impose on other road users as a result of congestion (see Glaister and Graham, 2004). Indeed, those with a low value of time can impose very costly delays on drivers with a high value of time.

Pricing has the potential to provide an efficient way of allocating scarce road space – in marked contrast to crude government charges such as fuel duties and vehicle taxes. Users who do not place a high value on travelling at peak times may be incentivised to travel at quieter times by cheaper off-peak toll rates. And motorists with a higher value of time can 'outbid' other drivers for delay-free journeys during peak hours. Importantly, pricing enables traffic levels to be managed to maximise capacity. When there is a risk of congestion, prices can be raised to choke off demand and ensure traffic flows freely. One key economic benefit is a reduced requirement for expensive new infrastructure to cope with peak-time demand. In other words, the introduction of pricing enables more efficient use of existing capacity.

Pricing also promotes efficient investment in new infrastructure. Prices provide valuable information about the preferences of road users. This information is vital for investment decisions, such as where to build additional road space (Day, 1998). High tolls will often be a signal that investment in new capacity would be profitable – although investors must also consider numerous other factors such as construction costs. Conversely, there would be little point in building road space in locations where toll rates were too low to make a commercial return. The price mechanism therefore helps ensure resources are allocated efficiently. Without pricing, investment is likely to be misallocated, although this may be mitigated to some extent by the deployment of cost–benefit analysis.

The two key benefits of road pricing – more efficient use of existing capacity and more efficient investment in new capacity – are likely to be undermined by government ownership. As discussed above, the incentives facing politicians and officials are very different from those of commercial businesses. In consequence, pricing under government ownership is likely to be determined by politics and bureaucratic imperatives rather than commercial criteria. Tolls will tend to be set at levels that are acceptable to key voting groups and special interests; administration costs will be inflated by self-interested officials; revenues will be diverted to pet projects (for example, tram schemes) for ideological reasons. These phenomena are all too evident in existing government road-pricing schemes, including the London Congestion Charge (see TfL, 2007). Political pricing overrides market pricing and the role of prices in coordinating the efficient use of resources is severely curtailed. The more widespread introduction of road pricing, while potentially beneficial, would not in itself solve the fundamental problems associated with government ownership of roads.

Are there compelling reasons for government ownership?

Despite the shortcomings, the great majority of roads remain under government ownership and management. Several arguments are used to justify this, including the idea that roads are public goods, concerns about the development of private monopolies and the observation that roads generate positive and negative externalities. Chapter 2 deals with these arguments, demonstrating that they are not valid objections to private ownership. But even if such economic objections can be addressed, there are practical arguments against transferring ownership to the private sector, for example concerns over access rights and the introduction of tolls. These issues are discussed in Chapter 3. While the process of denationalising roads may be complex in some instances, it is concluded that there are no practical obstacles that would prevent a gradual process of privatisation. The resulting economic benefits are also sketched out. The main barrier to action is therefore political.

Despite the numerous advantages of liberating roads from the state, policymakers may fear opposition from various interest groups. Yet there is evidence that politicians in several countries are becoming more receptive to the idea of privatising at least some roads. In the UK, for example, the prime minister has announced plans to allow private firms to lease motorways and trunk roads and to build new capacity, which could be tolled.[8] Moreover, the possibility of significant receipts from a sell-off is attractive for governments facing severe budget deficits. At the same time, technological improvements have enhanced the

8   In a speech on infrastructure to the Institute of Civil Engineering, 19 March 2012.

economic arguments for privatisation by lowering the transaction costs associated with road pricing. The growing number of successful privately built and operated roads around the world – often in developing countries – also strengthens the case for ending state control. Chapter 4 examines the political economy of transferring roads to private ownership. It shows how groups such as taxpayers, drivers and local residents would gain from the private ownership of roads and concludes that the very substantial efficiency gains derived from privatisation could offer significant rewards to policymakers bold enough to proceed with it. This is not to underestimate the size of the challenge. Calls for tight regulation of private enterprise dominate so-called market economies, and ill-defined notions of 'public interest' are used to justify the continued state provision of goods and services. Our findings suggest that this school of thought is flawed and we highlight the dangers and costs to society arising from its application to roads. The arguments in favour of privatisation are compelling.

2 STATE OWNERSHIP OR PRIVATE OWNERSHIP?

The general economic case against state ownership and in favour of privatisation was set out briefly in Chapter 1, and has been made in detail elsewhere (for example, Parker, 2009b). There are, however, specific questions related to roads in particular. This chapter addresses these issues and challenges the assumption that the ownership and/or management of roads are proper and necessary functions of the state.

Public versus private goods

It has often been argued that road networks are examples of 'public goods' (see Benson, 2004). This line of thought is, however, fundamentally flawed. Consideration of the two underlying requirements for a good or service to be described as a public good – the inability to exclude users and non-rivalry in consumption – suggests that road infrastructure is actually a private, not a public, good.[1]

Current motorway charging schemes, including penalties for non-compliance, clearly prove that drivers may be excluded from road use. Walter Block is straightforward in his assessment on excludability: 'There is nothing in principle to prevent

---

1   See Blankart (2006: 59) on the terminology.

excludability – there is only a lack of past history of market operation in this area and the limited powers of imagination on the part of economists' (Block, 2006: 105). It is often stated that, though applicable to motorways and country roads, the excludability would not be enforceable in city centres or residential areas. This argument is reminiscent of the debates in the 1980s when the technological possibility of automated road-user charging was questioned. Charging technology based on positioning systems such as GPS or mobile devices allows for precise localisation. Also, conurbations may provide a single tariff for different zones, such as for the entire city, for the centre, rings, feeder lanes, suburbs or residential areas, rather than point-to-point charging. Indeed, the Smeed Report published as early as 1964 clearly set out how charging could be applied efficiently even given the technology available then. Accordingly, at least one of the conditions – if not both of the conditions – of private goods is fulfilled.

In addition, congestion demonstrates that road users are often competing for scarce road space – there is therefore rivalry in consumption. Even where roads are not congested, they are not public goods but 'club goods'. The marginal cost of additional users may be trivial compared with the fixed cost of providing the road. Here, excludability still applies, but there is non-rivalry. The market can provide mechanisms of charging for club goods such as through annual subscriptions that give subscribers unlimited access rights for a period of time.

Internalisation of externalities

In addition to the debate about public goods, road infrastructure is commonly associated with positive or negative externalities.[2] Negative external effects include air pollution, noise and congestion. These are costs that are, for example, borne by residents next to a busy motorway, but are not taken into consideration by the individuals causing the externality, i.e. by the road operator and the road users.

There are, however, also positive externalities for which no transfer has so far been made, either.[3] Positive external effects include network benefits, such as the benefits to users of city roads that have been connected to the outside world by a motorway network, which might bring additional business opportunities and jobs (including to non-motorists), as well as more flexibility to travellers. In the same way, rural populations may benefit from connections to market their produce, commute to their city offices or enjoy cultural events in the nearby conurbation.

Now, recognising such externalities, road operators and residents may enter into private negotiation procedures. But, of course, high transaction costs place a burden on the negotiations for both parties. It is one of the alleged justifications for governmental activity that it may minimise transaction costs. However:

> It is clear that the government has powers which might
> enable it to get some things done at a lower cost than
> could a private organisation (or at any rate one without
> special governmental powers). But the governmental
> administrative machine is not itself costless. It can, in
> fact, on occasion be extremely costly. Furthermore,
> there is no reason to suppose that the restrictive and
> zoning regulations, made by a fallible administration

---

2   See Coase (1960) for a market approach on externalities without and with transaction costs involved.

3   Although estimates of such benefits may be included in project appraisals.

subject to political pressures and operating without any competitive check, will necessarily always be those which increase the efficiency with which the economic system operates. Furthermore, such general regulations which must apply to a wide variety of cases will be enforced in some cases in which they are clearly inappropriate. From these considerations it follows that direct governmental regulation will not necessarily give better results than leaving the problem to be solved by the market or the firm. ... There is, of course, a further alternative, which is to do nothing about the problem at all. And given that the costs involved in solving the problem by regulations issued by the governmental administrative machine will often be heavy (particularly if the costs are interpreted to include all the consequences which follow from the Government engaging in this kind of activity), it will no doubt be commonly the case that the gain which would come from regulating the actions which give rise to the harmful effects will be less than the costs involved in Government regulation. (Coase, 1960: 17–18)

The 'do nothing' option is the market solution and offers tailor-made solutions to road operators, users and residents alike. Whereas a rational road operator would negotiate with the users or owners of the city network regarding the positive externalities, residents next to a planned road or their representatives may ask for compensation to alleviate the negative externalities. This is obvious in the construction of new roads when an operator would price in externalities in order to pass them on to the road users as his customers. Transaction costs, though initially perhaps rather high, are likely to fall quickly, when residents concerned achieve economies by having their interests represented by associations, clubs or specialist legal representatives.

Contrary to the common assumption that private operators would neglect and run down the environment, it will thus become part of their utility function by private negotiations. By contrast, it is problematic to incorporate such goals in bureaucrats' utility function when running a state-owned, monopolistic road administration, although typically some attempt is made to estimate environmental externalities in the appraisal of new schemes.[4]

Market definition and segmentation

In a discussion on the current road administration or future road market it is necessary to assess possible market structures and the oft-cited threat of monopolistic tendencies in markets with high sunk costs. Does a private road industry tend to a monopolistic structure? And if so, would this justify state intervention or state ownership of such an industry?

Though a future road operator may enjoy exclusivity on, for example, the M1 between London and the Midlands, there are alternative transport options. These act, of course, as differentiated options rather than exact replicas. People can travel to the Midlands via the M40 or via A-roads – many of which are dual carriageway. An operator that is charging 'excessive' tolls on his road or offering inferior services is incentivising customers to switch to an alternative operator. There are also operators of competing modes of transport such as railways and, in some cases, coastal shipping and airlines. And some customers might substitute business travel with phone calls, video or online

---

4   In the absence of markets, it is difficult, if not impossible, to put accurate values on environmental externalities; particularly since individual valuations may be highly subjective (see Cordato, 2004).

conferences. Transport markets are closely interlinked and partly overlapping with other communications markets. Furthermore, this existing competition – perhaps already significantly greater than the competition that exists in other markets where there has been privatisation – is limited by the historical government road monopoly. High economic rents on a road would additionally signal other (potential) operators to consider competing for business and building new roads and alternative transport links.

Addressing these considerations, competition theory uses the concept of the relevant market that is clearly distinguishable from a material, spatial and temporal perspective (Schmidt, 1993: 44–9). Is the market scope local, regional, national, inter-regional or global? How dynamic is the market – are we dealing with a stable and stalled market or will it change over time? Is the market characterised by innovations that upset the current market structure and displace some of the industry or may wipe it out entirely? Taking an example from the early nineteenth century, the emergence of the railways turned the transport market upside down and accordingly faced strong opposition from turnpike owners, canal and sea-freight operators. But history repeated itself roughly a century later, when road and air industries presented a major challenge to the rail industry.[5]

It is rare in public policy to see nationalisation justified because private provision is, or could be, oligopolistic, and we should not accept that argument with regard to the road network either. Regulation of private monopolies is one way of dealing with problems of lack of competition (see later). There are, however,

---

5   See Knipping (2002: 29–32, 58–70) regarding opposition to the early railways in the UK and on the correlation of inter-modal road competition on the UK railway market during the interwar years.

other mechanisms too. Traditionally – especially in deregulated financial markets – ownership structures have emerged to deal with conflicts of interest between customers and owners, mutual insurers and banks being excellent examples. Ownership structures could also deal with the problems of monopolies in road ownership. There is no reason why roads could not be owned by trusts or organisations mainly governed by road users themselves, or owned by member organisations such as the former Automobile Association.[6]

Nonetheless, a denationalisation of the road industry should aim initially at creating smaller-sized lots of road networks than privatising the state monopoly in a single chunk, which would create a dominant position in the road market. Smaller sizes – whether area-based or route-based – would facilitate consolidation or deconsolidation moves in the road industry and shape something like an efficient market structure, save for the unavoidable inefficiencies and distortions that had been created by previous state monopoly.

State monopoly versus free-market choice

Monopolist means Single Seller. Literally therefore anyone is a monopolist who sells anything that is not in every respect, wrapping and location and service included, exactly like what other people sell: every grocer, or every haberdasher, or every seller of 'Good Humors' on a road that is not simply lined with sellers of the same brand of ice cream. This however is not what we mean when talking about monopolists. We mean only those single sellers whose markets are not open to the intrusion of would-be producers

---

6   This is discussed below.

of the same commodity and of actual producers of similar
ones or, speaking slightly more technically, only those single
sellers who face a given demand schedule that is severely
independent of their own action as well as of any reactions
to their action by other concerns. (Schumpeter, 1943: 98–9)

Schumpeter properly illustrates the fundamental characteristics of a monopoly, but first and foremost he highlights what
a monopoly is not. This is important because the term is often
deliberately used in a very loose and derogatory fashion in order
to denounce the advocates of the free market:

Economists, government agents, journalists and politicians
in this country obviously love the word because it has
come to be a term of opprobrium which is sure to rouse
the public's hostility against any interest so labelled. In
the Anglo-American world monopoly has been cursed and
associated with functionless exploitation ever since ... (ibid.:
100)

Schumpeter introduces the concept of potential competition when pointing towards the 'would-be producers of the same
commodity and of actual producers of similar' commodities. Both
groups are a potential threat to the monopoly – the higher the
monopoly rents, the bigger the incentive to challenge the monopolist. Also, he asserts that genuine long-run monopolies are hard
to defend in a competitive, dynamic market. Monopolists that do
not stay ahead of potential competitors in the market die a natural
death. In any case, temporary monopolies are far more common
than permanent ones. Indeed, they are a necessary incentive to
the entrepreneur and innovator who aims to harvest temporary
monopoly rents as reward for their entrepreneurial risk (Schumpeter, 1939: 102).

Following Schumpeter's definition of monopoly it would appear that monopolies are very, very rare – especially if monopolies depend on the non-existence of potential competition. We therefore need to ask how potential competition tends to be tamed in practice. In fact, legally sanctioned monopolies are generally the only incontestable monopolies – and thus monopolies in the above sense – against which not even the best potential innovation stands any chance.[7]

At the core of the contestability theory lies the concept of costless, reversible entry, as suggested by Baumol, Panzar and Willig:

> A perfectly contestable market is defined as one in which
> entry and exit are easy and costless, which may or may
> not be characterized by economies of scale or scope,
> but which has no entry barriers ... Potential entrants are
> assumed to face the same set of productive techniques and
> market demands as those available to incumbent firms.
> There are no legal restrictions on market entry or exit and
> no special costs that must be borne by an entrant that
> do not fall on incumbents as well. An entrepreneur will
> enter the market if he expects to obtain a positive profit by
> undercutting the incumbent's price and serving the entire
> market demand at the new lower price. If the incumbent
> readjusts his price, reducing it beneath that of the entrant,
> then the new competitor can readily exit from the market
> without loss of investment. Thus, potential entrants
> are undeterred by prospects of retaliatory price cuts by
> incumbents and instead are deterred only when the existing

---

7   Though critics may raise natural monopolies as incontestable, the authors contradict this charge. See, for example, Knipping (2002: 101–10, 314) for a more comprehensive assessment of (natural) monopolies, sunk costs and contestability and Baumol et al. (1982) for its theoretical construct.

market prices leave them no room for profitable entry ...
A contestable market need not be populated by a great
many firms: indeed, contestable markets may contain only
a single monopoly enterprise or they may be comprised of
duopolistic or oligopolistic firms. (Baumol et al., 1982: xx)

Thus, even if there is only a single seller serving a market, that market may still be contestable, as long as potential entrants bear costs that incumbents face as well. This is why contestable markets exhibit the same characteristics as perfectly competitive markets and lead to efficient market outcomes, notwithstanding the number of producers of the same good in the same market.

The availability of sustainable prices *does* permit the
incumbent to preclude entry. But he can do so *only* by
offering the public the very same benefits that actual
competition would otherwise have brought with it. With
entry barriers, supernormal profits, inefficiencies, cross
subsidies, and nonoptimal prices all become possible. But
in a contestable market, which is perfectly consistent with
the presence of fixed costs that are not sunk, matters change
drastically, and government intervention can contribute
far less, if anything, to the general welfare. (Ibid.: 292–3,
emphasis in the original)

The sunk costs of road infrastructure are obviously a barrier to costless reversible entry, since new entrants are likely to incur costs that incumbents have already borne. It is here that we need to re-examine the scope of the market in order to understand that road operators are not the only market participants that have sunk investments. The same applies to the neighbouring rail and country-road operators and the competing operators of parallel highway routes. Moreover, market entrants may disregard an incumbent's sunk costs if they are not entering the same market but outwit the incumbent by offering safer, faster and more energy efficient roads, for example with exclusive truck lanes; optimised construction works at night; well-lit and ice-free roads; a shorter, more direct connection; an innovative asphalt surface; customer-oriented pricing schemes; automatic guiding and traffic sign recognition via a vehicle's on-board unit, and so on. Indeed, in some cases it may be more costly to 'retrofit' innovations to existing infrastructure than to include them with new roads, giving entrants an advantage over incumbents. And this is just an appetiser of what a free market in roads might bring, depending on each entrepreneur and his vision. We know what a statist, monopolistic road administration looks like already.[8]

According to Demsetz, 'The key to monopoly power is the ability of an industry to restrict or retard the expansion and utilization of productive capacity. Government can offer to industry much greater powers of coercion to accomplish this end than can be supplied by the industry itself' (Demsetz, 1989: 108). He concludes that 'government intervention that has created and sustained monopoly should be our primary target' (ibid.: 109).

In the road industry, we are currently dealing with a legally protected monopoly under public ownership. It is mistaken to assume that this means that the monopolistic structure is necessarily a feature of road provision. In fact, market provision and operation have deliberately been excluded and crowded out by state ownership (see, for example, Plowden, 1971). As public

---

8   This is not to say there has been a complete absence of innovation on state-owned roads. For example, high-occupancy lanes have been introduced in the USA and active traffic management in the UK. Nevertheless, the scope for innovation and entrepreneurship has been extremely limited.

supply of existing infrastructure does not necessarily reflect customers' demand, the system might be inefficient if it were simply sold to private investors as it is constructed. This mismatch is by no means a market failure, but must be assigned to the government ownership of the existing road network (Knipping, 2005: 99). It is at individual governments' discretion to continue running road networks as state monopolies or to replace the incontestable single seller with the market's innovative potential.

In summary, a complex problem is oversimplified when arguments relating to natural monopoly are used to justify the nationalisation of roads. A fundamental point about the extent of the market is misunderstood – the relevant market, for example, is not a particular motorway but all the different ways of travelling to a particular destination. Secondly, potential competition is as important as actual competition. Finally, nationalisation is, in any case, not the best way of providing goods and services even where there is monopoly power.

Does private ownership imply a specific pricing model?

Economists have long taken an interest in efficient road pricing. However revealing such debates may be for economic modelling, these pricing schemes usually presuppose state ownership of road networks and, in many respects, they resemble 'market socialism' in that they use textbook models to try to find efficient pricing models under nationalisation. It is one of the objectives of this monograph to move the discussion towards the concept of a market for roads.

No economic model can simulate the market outcome that would have developed in the absence of state intervention in the transport market. Though models might derive an optimal road market in a theoretical economy under *ceteris paribus* conditions, it would not reflect the complexity of the real-world road market. And as we do not know the optimal market structure and outcome, we should be wary of repeating the mistakes of the past by planning and administering markets. In other words, for road pricing schemes to work effectively, we need to denationalise roads so that the market can develop appropriate pricing models.

Hayek warned of falling into the trap of what he coined 'scientistic' errors, meaning the attempt to apply the tools and methods from exact natural sciences in the social sciences:

> Unlike the position that exists in the physical sciences, in economics and other disciplines that deal with essentially complex phenomena, the aspects of the events to be accounted for about which we can get quantitative data are necessarily limited and may not include the important ones. While in the physical sciences it is generally assumed ... that any important factor which determines the observed events will itself be directly observable and measurable, in the study of such complex phenomena as the market, which depend on the actions of many individuals, all the circumstances which will determine the outcome of a process ... will hardly ever be fully known or measurable. And while in the physical sciences the investigator will be able to measure what ... he thinks important, in the social sciences often that is treated as important which happens to be accessible to measurement. (Hayek, 1974)

Closely related to this point is the point made by Austrian competition economists – taking their lead from Hayek – that a market is necessary in order to discover what the outcome of a competitive process would be. Without that competitive process, the outcome – in this case a system and set of road prices – cannot simply be computed.

Even if the technical problem of determining the appropriate level and structure of road prices could be solved, it would be impossible to prevent political interests taking priority if the pricing of roads were left to politicians – indeed, this has been the experience of the London road pricing scheme.

If market forces are to be applied to road networks that have mostly been in the public domain for centuries, governments and their agents should simply withdraw. Should governments prefer to follow their conventional wisdom and implant political objectives into privatisation schemes, the process may end up even more distorted than the current statism. Realistically, governments will aim to maximise the receipts for the public purse while observing their re-election constraint. Unfortunately, this would distort any denationalisation process, leading to failure that would eventually be blamed on private business. This happened in the process of rail privatisation:

> Moreover, during a privatisation process, governments
> are usually eager to ensure that their political interests
> are properly represented in a market to be designed – and
> thus, their lobbies satisfied and their re-election ensured.
> The privatisation of British Rail was a telling example: the
> privatisation process was undermined from the outset
> due to government meddling. (Knipping, 2002: 232–7;
> Knipping, 2006: 164–9)

In order for a road and transport market to take shape, market forces should be allowed to operate freely, rather than being hampered by rules and regulations considered desirable by bureaucrats, lobbyists and politicians. We deal with the actual transition from state administration to market in the next chapter. Owing to current government ownership, such a transition to private ownership requires some set of rules that will be imposed by the current owners of the roads. These rules should be as non-interventionist as possible. Any negative side effects of a tightly regulated privatisation process are likely to be the fault of government, not of private business. They will represent examples of 'government failure' rather than of market failure. The next chapter sets out various options for privatising already existing roads or road networks, such as a sale or auction, or distributing the roads to taxpayers, road users or residents, whether free of charge or for a price. That chapter also deals with initial allotment or network sizes of the future road operators.

Once the road operators are up and running, they will be free to determine their own approach to pricing. They might decide to follow suggestions from economists on efficient road pricing for their network. They may implement GPS-based charging systems on their road networks according to which drivers would pay for their actual road usage (see Box 3). GPS-based systems can offer differentiated tariffs according to the time of day and congestion levels, thus providing an efficient mechanism to manage traffic flows (Knipping, 2011). Operators may also offer flat-rate tariffs, prepaid packages, commuter schemes, car-sharing packages, monthly or annual subscription fees and so on. Rather than using GPS technology, some operators may revert to toll gates as traditionally used in many countries to date, or indeed offer customers more than one charging option.[9] Others, however, may even decide to offer free usage during certain times of the day to

---

9   Many existing tolled highways offer electronic cashless and traditional cash tolls.

induce users to travel off peak, ease congestion during peak traffic and increase the competitiveness of their networks during peak times, or just as a marketing strategy. Alternatively, roads could also be financed by advertising posters, electronic commercials or sponsorship.

This list is not exclusive and hardly could be, as entrepreneurs or marketing and pricing departments of operators may come up with new pricing schemes. Such innovations in pricing are, however, only possible through a competition in ideas, notwithstanding the ideas that bureaucrats or economists may think reasonable or calculate as welfare maximising. That is the difference from government ownership – private ownership offers choice and options in pricing schemes that are to be decided by the entrepreneur in response to customers' demands. Efficient pricing is the result of a competitive market, whereby a myriad of decisions based on dispersed knowledge is coordinated. As stated in Hayek's Nobel Prize lecture:

> It is indeed the source of the superiority of the market order ... when it is not suppressed by the powers of government ... that in the resulting allocation of resources more of the knowledge of particular facts will be utilised which exists only dispersed among uncounted persons, than any one person can possess. But because we, the observing scientists, can thus never know all the determinants of such an order, and in consequence also cannot know at which particular structure of prices and wages demand would everywhere equal supply, we also cannot measure the deviations from that order ... (Hayek, 1974)

Box 3 **Toll Collect – electronic toll charging in Germany**
Toll Collect GmbH, a joint venture of the German Daimler
AG, Deutsche Telekom AG and French Cofiroute, runs the
German motorway toll charging system that is based on
the global positioning system (GPS).* The tolls are payable
by all trucks of more than twelve tonnes on about 12,000
kilometres of federal motorways and 1,000 kilometres of
trunk roads. The company commenced operations on 1
January 2005 following an auction and thus became the
world's first operator of a toll charging system for trucks
based on GPS.

The system operates both via an automatic log-on with
On-Board Units that Toll Collect provides and with a manual
pre-booking process of roads via an online platform or toll
terminals. Operators that rarely use the German road network
usually prefer the manual log-on. To date, more than 665,000
On-Board Units for automatic toll collection have been
installed, with 43.5 per cent registered outside Germany.
Tolls are calculated based on the emission class and number
of axles on the truck and on the distance travelled on the toll
route. The Federal Trunk Road Toll Act assigns each vehicle
to one of four categories, based on its emission class. These
toll rates mean that trucks with the latest-generation exhaust
systems and those that have been upgraded with particle

Signalling effects of market prices and market allocation

State-owned road networks are plagued by persistent and predict-
able delays – for example, during public holidays. Pricing could
allocate traffic flows more efficiently, smoothing traffic jams,

reduction systems pay significantly less than high-emission vehicles.[†] According to this principle Toll Collect's rates (at the time of writing) range from €0.141 to €0.288 per kilometre, depending on emission class and axles.

Toll Collect offers a free-flow charging system that does not require any stops at toll booths that would cause delays and traffic jams. According to Toll Collect, the company '... was tasked with setting up and operating an electronic toll collection system for heavy freight traffic in Germany'. Note that, as such, Toll Collect procures revenue for the federal budget but the rates do not necessarily match those that a private entrepreneur might ask for on a privately owned and operated road network, not least because the scheme charges tolls only for heavy goods vehicles.

The collection system illustrates, however, how road pricing could be implemented in a private road market – technology certainly is not a major obstacle to denationalising the road industry. The flexibility of such a system allows the introduction of various additional services such as telematics and further rates, whether due to time of the day or season, speed, special discounts or even weather conditions.

[*] The data on Toll Collect is based exclusively on publicly available information from Toll Collect GmbH on www.toll-collect.de
[†] www.toll-collect.de as of 15 September 2011.

while preventing road accidents and fatalities at the same time.

Notwithstanding the motivations – or even the well-intended goals – of state planners or political decision-makers, road networks lack an efficient allocation of scarce resources. This is a natural consequence of state control and ownership. The government's roads budget is determined in a political process competing with other politically determined budgets such as defence, health, education, and so on. The relationship between this process and the needs of roads users is tenuous. For example, in order to keep costs down, state authorities in charge of road networks may prefer to have construction sites in operation during normal working hours only to save heavy mark-ups for night shifts. When construction work is taken up in the morning in time for the commuter traffic, the negative externality hits only the commuters, not the state or road budget. In a state-owned road system, the cost of such inconvenience is likely to affect voting behaviours only in extreme conditions, and so the incentive for politicians to reflect the views of road users in their decisions is limited. Indeed, if there is no charging mechanism, even if road users would like to pay the extra cost of night-working themselves, so that they can have a less congested road, they cannot do so. The additional cost of night-working would be borne by taxpayers in general. There is no mechanism for signalling road users' preferences, nor for responding to those preferences. Exactly the same argument applies to poor road surfaces, pothole repairs and so on.

As such, even if bureaucrats 'mean well', they will not 'know well' – they cannot know the preferences of road users even if they want to satisfy those preferences. At best road users get what bureaucrats think they want – and this only if there are sufficient resources from the government budget and if policy is not determined by the preferences of other interest groups.

Implementing market pricing on the roads with competing road operators addresses the causes, rather than dealing only with the symptoms, of badly run roads. The superiority of the pricing system lies in its signalling capability both to customers and to operators of a road network. If users perceive prices as too high, they will look for other options, whether that is car sharing, a shift to off-peak journeys, other routes provided by competing operators or even a switch to other modes of transportation.

On the other side of the equation, road operators can allocate traffic flows more efficiently across their network by pricing differently depending on the time of day or available capacity. They may build express lanes for customers willing to pay extra for a guaranteed traffic-jam-free journey. Some operators may offer ice-free or illuminated roads, others may operate traffic signs that communicate with the car's on-board computer, run separate truck lanes to increase road safety and reduce journey times for car drivers or use innovative asphalt to reduce traction for higher energy efficiency. In order to keep their road network in a shape that attracts customers, construction is unlikely to occur during peak commuting hours, when operators receive the largest chunk of their revenue. Rather, construction could be expected to take place during off-peak hours and operators may revert to intense construction at night in order to have the roads open for undisturbed morning traffic. Again, the price signals arising from the profitability of charging structures for different approaches will provide much more effective information on the value of different services to road users than the political process.

The pricing system assists the road operator in making choices to maximise the shareholders' return:

> It enables entrepreneurs, by watching the movement of comparatively few prices, as an engineer watches the hands of a few dials, to adjust their activities to those of their fellows. The important point here is that the price system

will fulfil this function only if competition prevails, that
is, if the individual producer has to adapt himself to price
changes and cannot control them. The more complicated
the whole, the more dependent we become on that division
of knowledge between individuals whose separate efforts are
co-ordinated by the impersonal mechanism for transmitting
the relevant information known by us as the price system.
(Hayek, 1944: 36–7)

The powerful role of special interests in determining policy
under a nationalised roads system is precisely due to governments' legal monopoly. Even after a privatisation that cedes all
power to build, maintain and operate the roads, governments and
their agents may still impose new sets of rules on the operators.
These may come in the form of safety standards, speed limits, new
taxes and fees, licences for the construction of new roads, price
controls or environmental regulations that may impact the entire
road industry or individual companies. A market that is, however,
subjected to a catalogue of actual and potential rules and regulations as a consequence of interest group influence cannot be
expected to release the full potential of a free market. The more
decisions that are not influenced by price signals, the less innovative the sector will be.

Interaction between road transport and other segments of the transport market

As already noted, the road market is one segment of the wider
transport market. The market for transport includes other means
of transportation, such as rail, air and shipping, but overlaps
with other sectors such as communications. Modern means

of communication, such as the Internet, video and telephone conferences, may already have reduced the number of necessary journeys and will most likely do so even further in the future.

Accordingly, even if the current state-run road operators exercise monopoly power in the road industry providing suboptimal services, customers may still vote with their feet and switch between modes. Nonetheless, the road users have a welfare loss, because they are using a second-choice mode. Thus, inter-modal competition only partially restrains monopolistic behaviour, especially when the whole road network is owned by government.

In many respects, a government monopolist is also worse than a private monopolist – though we dispute the idea that a private monopolist would emerge in a privatised roads system, even ignoring inter-modal competition. As long as the operator is in government ownership, it does not have to react to market signals, such as a slump in road-user numbers – indeed, in the absence of prices, there are limited signals to which to respond. On the contrary, an inter-modal split in favour of modes other than cars might be politically triggered.[10] A private operator could not ignore such signals and would have to react by addressing customers' reasons for switching to other modes, irrespective of the political fashions of the day.

In order to get the transport market to work, a market organisation is required across the entire transport sector. Taking a highly subsidised railway market as an example, some road

10 Süddeutsche Zeitung (2011): the prime minister designate of the German state of Baden Württemberg, Winfried Kretschmann from the Green Party, reportedly suggested that it would be better to have fewer cars rather than more. According to Kretschmann, comprehensive mobility concepts are required that embrace running, cycling, driving cars and riding trains. He suggested that smart networks would be needed.

Box 4 **Privatisation and 'integration'**

It is often contended that state intervention is required to 'integrate' different transport modes. Indeed, this was an important theme of the 1997 Labour government. In one sense 'integration' refers to bringing different modes under some degree of central control to pursue centrally determined objectives. The shortcomings of this form of integration have been discussed at length elsewhere in this monograph. In another sense, however, integration is simply understood as meaning coordination – for example, the 'clockwork' precision of trains, buses and trams sometimes seen in Switzerland.

It is often assumed that market forces are unable to achieve integration of the latter type. Yet there is substantial evidence to suggest that privately owned transport networks may be highly successful at coordinating different modes. For example, private railways in Japan operate extensive bus and taxi services which feed into their rail networks. These private firms also integrate their transport services with land-use planning, for example by developing housing estates, offices, shopping centres and leisure facilities adjacent to railway stations. This benefits passengers by providing new amenities in convenient locations and benefits the railways by increasing ridership.

Similarly, the private railways of nineteenth-century Britain built goods depots and wholesale markets at major

users would switch to trains owing to artificially lowered prices if they bore the full cost of road use at the margin. Not only will the subsidy bill have to be borne by taxpayers; the switching termini so that freight could be offloaded and distributed across cities via horse-drawn wagons. And they often went to great lengths to ensure that their passengers could easily reach their final destination. In the 1850s the Great Western Railway and the Great Northern Railway joined forces to part-fund the construction of the Metropolitan Railway, the world's first underground passenger railway. The line linked termini at Paddington, Euston and King's Cross to Farringdon Street on the edge of the City. It slashed journey times from Paddington to just eighteen minutes, compared with around an hour by other modes; reduced fares, compared with omnibuses, by a factor of five; and carried 12 million people in its first full year of operation (see Wolmar, 2004).

In reality, private transport operators have strong economic incentives to improve connectivity to other modes. By reducing door-to-door travel times, they can encourage more people to use their services. There is no contradiction between privatisation and coordination. Indeed, market pricing enables different services to be coordinated in an efficient manner. Private road owners can therefore be expected to coordinate their services with other transport modes in order to attract travellers and increase toll revenues. For example, they might decide to construct park-and-ride facilities on the edge of major cities or even run peak-time bus services for drivers unable to afford the toll rates.

customers would suffer their welfare loss in addition. Also, the road operators, car manufacturers and suppliers would be hit, resulting in crowding out of private initiative and investments.

The transport sector depends on network infrastructures that are characterised by high sunk costs. Whereas central planning boards, such as the British Transport Commission, were created to coordinate the transport industry, inter-modal market allocation was neglected. Operators' services frequently depend on interlinking and coordinating with other networks. Freight planes or container ships without rail and road links would defy their purpose, while roads that lead to nowhere or offer no connections would quickly see few users without a legally sanctioned monopoly. Although it is frequently thought that 'integration' requires central political control, the opposite is the case (see Box 4).

Private ownership versus compromise models

Lobbyists, though, are professionals in selling ideas. It is likely that they will manage to defend and secure their principal's interests to a certain extent when moving from a state road administration to a road market.

In a discussion on the size of government, Mueller finds that

> ... government bureaucracies do have higher unit costs than private firms when they supply measurable outputs, such as tons of garbage collected. Borcherding ... describes this as 'the Bureaucratic Rule of Two' – 'removal of an activity from the private sector will double its unit costs of production.' If unit costs rise by this much when direct comparisons with private sector alternatives are possible, how much more are they inflated when the bureaucracy knows it cannot be subjected to a comparison with private market alternatives? (Mueller, 1996: 340)[11]

---

11   Quoting from Borcherding (1977: 62).

Many roads were once owned privately. What has been taken from the private sector and reorganised in a state monopoly should be returned to the private sector in a way that enables the market to operate freely – meticulous, 'scientistic' market planning would lead back into the command economy in road transport provision. What the market structure would have looked like if road networks had not been developed by governments is, however, impossible to ascertain. The next chapter explains how to release road networks into the market economy without predetermining their fate by prescribing a market structure.

To the authors' knowledge, there has not yet been a privatisation in which the state took a minimalistic approach to regulation and market distortion. Assuming today's mixed economies rather than a 'state of nature' as a starting point, we acknowledge that governments will play a significant role in the privatisation process. Thus, their decision-makers need to be convinced to proceed with a clean-cut process, rather than one of the compromise models that rent-seekers will try hard to sell.

The choice of most governments that embrace private elements in road provisioning has, up to the current day, mostly resulted in various middle-of-the-road approaches that may include tolling, privately built roads, privately operated or financed roads or some degree of public–private partnership. None of the existing schemes, however, is based on private roads that are privately planned and financed, built, run and regulated. Whereas full business risks are borne by private entrepreneurs in the latter case, governance may not be congruent with ownership in compromise approaches. Such disparity necessarily leads to market distortions and network inefficiencies, as projects will be approved according to political considerations that would not have gone ahead were they decided purely according to market and, thus, customer preferences.

Mixed governance structures – whether related to public corporations or mixed economies – lack transparency and a clear responsibility for the use of the funds provided by taxpayers. Essentially we are facing a principal–agent problem, where the principals have no direct means of control over the agents.[12]

In order to align their interests and reinstate the principals' control over their agents, the principals must be enabled to sanction the behaviour of the management. This can be achieved by denationalising the assets and returning them to private ownership. This process is usually referred to as privatisation or denationalisation.

---

12 Blankart (2006: 531–53) describes the two-tier principal–agent problem in bureaucracies, with the voters as principals; the politicians and their bureaucrats represent the two tiers of agents that do not necessarily maximise their principals' but their own utility. The problem is increased in the case of state bureaucracies that are legal monopolies.

3 A FREE MARKET IN ROADS

Chapter 2 demonstrated that the economic arguments in favour of state-owned roads are weak. It also showed how we might expect government roads to be marked by a high degree of inefficiency and government failure. But the process of transferring roads to private ownership is challenging. There are difficult issues to resolve regarding property access, competition, the planning of new routes and the transaction costs associated with pricing. This chapter assesses the practical policy options available for privatisation. It draws on evidence from case studies from around the world. Entrepreneurs and communities have already discovered solutions to many of the practical difficulties that have been raised as objections to privatisation.

Different types of road present different problems, so the discussion is organised accordingly. The privatisation process, competition issues, regulation and pricing technologies are examined. Further problems that apply to all roads, such as the fiscal and legal framework, are discussed at the end of this chapter.

Motorways

The privatisation of motorways and motorway-style trunk roads is relatively straightforward compared with that associated with other types of road. They generally do not provide direct access to property, so associated access issues are not a constraint. Nevertheless, policymakers would face a series of key decisions when privatising motorway networks, including the mechanism by which ownership is transferred, whether networks should be split up, the timescale and so on. Further questions include the extent to which private motorways should be subject to state regulation.

The privatisation process

Various transfer mechanisms would be available to governments wishing to denationalise motorways. These include a flotation process similar to that undertaken with other nationalised industries that have been privatised in recent decades (see Parker, 2009b). Considerable sums could potentially be raised through such a process. For example, the UK motorway network has been valued at around £100 billion (Mulheirn and Furness, 2010: 15). The process of valuing the network is highly problematic, however. The value of the assets is contingent on numerous government interventions, including tax rates, regulation, subsidies to competing transport modes, planning controls and so on. And clearly there are strong incentives for governments to maximise receipts from the sale. Perhaps the biggest danger is regulation that stifles competition from new routes in order to minimise the revenue risks facing potential buyers. At the same time, politicians would face strong pressures to protect consumers from economic charging, such as motorists who use particular routes to travel to work. As discussed in Chapter 2, a heavily regulated form of privatisation would destroy many of the economic benefits. Indeed, the benefits could be outweighed by additional transaction costs.[1]

As well as the economic arguments, there is the question of 'restorative justice' or restitution (Carnis, 2001). Motorways were generally built on land compulsorily purchased from owners, while their construction and maintenance have been paid for by taxpayers. It is arguably objectionable for governments to benefit from the sale of such assets. Such objections could be mitigated, however, if the receipts were used to cut taxes. Earmarking for tax cuts could also reduce the incentives for regulation discussed above and help overcome political opposition.

Giving away motorways, for example through the distribution of free shares, is an alternative option to a sale. A key advantage is that there is no technical need to value the assets, avoiding some of the incentives for state intervention associated with their sale. A key difficulty, however, is how to allocate the shares. If free shares were given to every citizen, this would not reflect the amount of tax they had paid to fund the construction and maintenance of the network. At the other extreme, if shares were given to the original owners of the land (or their heirs) the value of the assets transferred would far exceed the original value of the 'unimproved land'.[2] Allocating a high proportion of shares to vehicle owners might be a reasonable approximation, with allocations perhaps depending on vehicle size to take account of different

1   For an introduction to transaction-cost economics, see Williamson (2008). Some would argue that the benefits of rail privatisation were outweighed by the transactions costs arising from the particular method of privatisation chosen.

2   The issue is further complicated because landowners generally received compensation when their land was nationalised, although this does not change the fact that it was typically taken without their consent. In many countries, however, the owners' ancestors may have stolen the land, for example from indigenous peoples. Land restitution is never likely to be a straightforward process.

amounts of motoring taxes paid. Heavy goods vehicles, though more highly taxed, are also responsible for a disproportionate amount of damage to motorways, so their owners' allocations could be adjusted downwards accordingly. It might be objected that the widely dispersed ownership resulting from a 'share giveaway' would prevent shareholders from effectively controlling the company managers – an example of the principal–agent problem in corporate governance (see, for example, Butler (2011) and Ellerman (2001)). Provided there were no controls on the sale of shares, however, it seems likely that financial institutions would soon be able to accumulate significant shareholdings.

A third option would be to transfer ownership into some kind of non-governmental institution. Newbery (1998), for example, has suggested that many of the deficiencies of nationalised roads in the UK could be remedied through the creation of a new company to manage the network, which he calls Roadtrack. This could replace the Highways Agency, the government agency that manages trunk roads and motorways, and would in essence be a regulated utility, overseen by a body termed Ofroad. The regulated utility model would prevent many of the benefits of a less controlled, more free-market approach. Nevertheless, it should not be ruled out as a useful stepping stone between the current state-centred framework and private ownership. A regulated utility might face less political opposition and could detach motorways from reliance on central government funding for repairs and improvements.

A further possible institutional structure for motorways would be to transfer ownership to a new generation of turnpike trusts.[3] These would charge tolls to cover the costs of maintenance

---

3   See Albert (1972) for an introduction to the turnpike trusts of eighteenth- and nineteenth-century Britain.

and improvements, and could be constituted for the benefit of the road users. Such organisations could be appropriate for some existing motorways, although the absence of strong entrepreneurial incentives is a clear disadvantage. The RAC or the AA, as they used to be constituted before demutualisation, are examples of the sorts of organisations that could form such trusts.

Different approaches have different net benefits in different situations, and it is important that these are carefully considered before privatisation – or at least to establish that it is possible to transfer from one form of ownership model to another. For example, member-owned organisations are often more prone to principal–agent problems and find it more difficult to raise capital than limited companies. Limited companies, on the other hand, may be less satisfactory for the management of routes where there is more monopoly power.

Price regulation and competition

Market prices transmit vital information to road owners, helping them decide where to invest and how to maximise revenues by preventing congestion. There is thus a strong case to allow owners to determine prices without any controls by government. Price regulations lead to the misallocation of resources (see, for example, Kates, 2011: 119–22). For example, price capping could undermine investment in new capacity while at the same time increasing congestion. Nevertheless, policymakers may well argue that motorway owners could exploit their market power by 'overcharging' users and that regulation is therefore justified.

There are several responses to this approach. First, it should be observed that traffic is not price inelastic (Graham and Glaister,

2004). As tolls rise, traffic falls, and it is irrational for road owners to charge higher tolls than the revenue-maximising point. Secondly, profit-maximising owners would have to bear in mind the wider economic impact of their charges. The spatial pattern of economic activity is fluid and responsive to changes in transport costs. Road owners will tend to benefit from attracting economic activity into the areas served by their infrastructure and will lose revenues if businesses locate elsewhere as a result of uncompetitive tolls. Owners face the prospect of competition from other modes of transport (e.g. rail, air, pipeline and shipping) as well as from new roads constructed by entrepreneurs. There are therefore significant incentives for road owners to maintain their prices at competitive levels. Even a single owner (i.e. a road monopolist) would not be immune to these feedbacks. Moreover, as discussed in Chapter 2, there is strong economic evidence that persistent monopolies are either an efficient market response to transaction costs or, more likely, the result of artificial barriers to market entry created by state intervention. Of course, the strict planning policies of many countries would represent a very serious barrier to entry in roads markets, an issue discussed in more detail in the section below on new roads. Finally, it should be noted, too, that there may be mechanisms other than state regulation for dealing with potential monopolies, such as an ownership structure whereby the users have the opportunity also to be owners.

Competition issues would be a factor in the decision whether to privatise or transfer a network to the private sector as a single entity or divided into several units. While the former option might be expected to present problems associated with monopoly, the latter might be affected by higher transaction costs and fewer economies of scale. Entrepreneurs operating in unhampered markets are generally best placed to discover the most efficient structure, suggesting that the initial nature of the transfer may be less important than the absence of controls on the structure of the industry and the removal of artificial barriers to market entry. The privatisation of British Rail demonstrated the disadvantages of government imposing a fixed structure on an industry (see Tyrrall, 2004).

Road-pricing technologies

The introduction of pricing on motorways risks imposing significant transaction costs. Conventional toll booths slow traffic down and may be expensive to introduce, particularly on routes with multiple exits, or impractical for certain locations where there is no room to accommodate the additional width typically required. The scope for variable pricing may also be limited with this option. Nevertheless, toll booths are relatively low cost and could be particularly suitable for uncongested rural motorways. They are widely used across the world and the technology is tried and tested. They can also be combined with other technologies such that the toll booths are one payment option among several, perhaps aimed primarily at occasional users.

Another low-tech charging option would be some kind of disc displayed on vehicles' windscreens to demonstrate that user fees had been paid. For example, in Switzerland and several other countries[4] motorway users must buy a sticker called a 'vignette'. Any driver not displaying a valid sticker may be fined by the police. Private road owners could operate similar schemes,

4   For example, Austria, Hungary, Romania, Slovakia and Slovenia.

although they may be unsuitable for charging many different toll rates according to the time of day. In addition, flat-fee systems tend to incentivise heavy usage and discriminate against occasional drivers – although this may be appropriate where there are large fixed costs. Nevertheless, there is scope for entrepreneurs to develop more refined systems.

Simple electronic pricing systems include the use of tags, which charge motorists when they drive past certain charge points. Alternatively, Automatic Number Plate Recognition (ANPR) may be employed, as with the London Congestion Charge system. This is a costly way of charging for entry into an urban zone as an extensive network of cameras covering every route is required. It would be much more straightforward, however, to use ANPR on motorways, where there are relatively few entry and exit points. A key advantage is that vehicles themselves need not be fitted with charging technology. There may, however, be high enforcement costs related to unregistered and falsely registered vehicles. To some extent ANPR may be inconvenient for occasional users if it requires them to pay online or over the phone.

Perhaps the most sophisticated pricing systems are based on satellite tracking. Such a system would enable very comprehensive schemes because there is no need to create charging infrastructure on minor roads. Highly nuanced pricing regimes are also possible. Once the technology is fitted to vehicles, the inconvenience is minimal, with users sent a bill based on their use of the network. As with mobile phones, network access could also be available through pre-payment/pay-as-you-go options. Operators could offer discounts for pre-booked off-peak users, deploying similar demand management strategies to rail operators and no-frills airlines. Key disadvantages include the potentially high cost of supplying and fitting 'black boxes' to cars and administering schemes. In the UK it has been estimated that each box could cost several hundred pounds.[5] A complex, IT-driven road pricing scheme could also be subject to the cost overruns that have plagued similar projects. Having said this, it seems likely that technology costs will fall over time. And private road owners would of course have strong incentives to keep costs down (unlike state administrators, who are likely to be captured by producer interests). It may even be possible to use existing infrastructure for charging, such as mobile phone SIM cards. A more intractable problem may be the implications of vehicle tracking for civil liberties. Governments already use ANPR cameras, public transport smart cards and mobile phone records to monitor their citizens. Satellite tracking would add a new dimension to the surveillance state. Data protection laws could help assuage fears, although it seems unlikely that government security services could be trusted to adhere strictly to such legislation. The private ownership of roads would at least create a barrier between such data and government bureaucracies, and, given an appropriate legal framework, privacy agreements could be part of the contract between owners and road users, such as is the case with banks and insurance companies.

Finally, there may be situations where motorway owners decide not to charge tolls. Perhaps a stretch of motorway provides access to a major retail centre or leisure development whose owners decide that free road space will help attract customers (in the same way that free parking is often provided).

Private ownership would facilitate a market discovery process

---

5   See   http://www.telegraph.co.uk/news/uknews/1543111/Drivers-face-600-bill-for-an-in-car-road-pricing-black-box.html

to find the most efficient ways of charging for road use where applicable. Accordingly, it is important that governments avoid prescribing road pricing techology through regulation. In this context it is regrettable that the European Union has imposed a directive on the interoperability of charging systems, which requires:

> that electronic road charging and toll systems should be technically and contractually interoperable i.e. that there should be a Europe-wide mechanism to ensure that all charge operators exchange information so that users of a range of tolling and charging services across Europe can register with a single service provider of their choice and use a single on-board unit to access all charging schemes within the EU. (DfT, 2004: ch. 5)

Such legislation could severely hamper the market process by which entrepreneurs develop efficient charging mechanisms and business structures.

It would, however, be undesirable if road operators were prevented from cooperating on charging technology, leading to a needless variety in approaches taken by different road operators. Private railway companies did, of course, see the benefits of cooperation and introduced through-ticketing in the nineteenth century. It is very important that competition authorities do not prevent cooperation with regard to charging methods.

Major roads

Major roads carry large volumes of traffic but, unlike motorways and motorway-style trunk roads, they also provide access to adjacent properties. There may also be long-standing rights of way for bicycles, horses, pedestrians and so on – users who currently may not pay anything to use the road space.

The privatisation process

The privatisation process would have to take full account of these access issues. An important concern would be that road owners could restrict access rights in order to expropriate property. For example, if a farmer could reach his property only by using a particular route, the owners of that road could potentially render the farm worthless by denying access. Thus, as part of the privatisation process, a contract would have to be drawn up, guaranteeing rights of passage to affected property owners – though some of these might come under common law obligations. This might cause problems for the road owners, since farmers, for example, could create congestion with their vehicles. Of course, these difficulties are already commonplace under the state system, and at least the market would provide incentives for road owners to negotiate to limit access rights for an appropriate level of compensation to spare other users the inconvenience and danger of agricultural vehicles.

For reasons of safety and efficiency, access rights contracts would have to include restrictions on the type and size of vehicles allowed on the relevant road. Potential problems arise from this, since it is difficult to predict what kind of technology will be available, say, 50 years in the future. In the nineteenth century access rights may have specified that access would be allowed for pedestrians, pedal cycles and horse-drawn vehicles. By 1950 these rights would have been seriously devalued through the advent of the motor car, possibly allowing road owners to purchase land at very low rates where no car access rights existed. One possible solution is to insert a clause in the contract referring to something like 'the hegemonic transport technology of the day', which would be determined in the future by an arbitrator agreed by both parties in the event of a dispute.

Perhaps the trickiest issue of all is how far 'residential' access rights should be extended. In large urban areas there could be several business districts and numerous residential areas, with a complex web of major roads connecting them. The difficulties should not be exaggerated, since in the long term they would be mitigated by the growth of new infrastructure without such inherited problems (see below).

Price regulation and competition

Beyond the matters discussed in the section on motorways, which are also relevant to major roads, access issues may also impact on pricing regimes. To some extent, residents of adjoining property may represent a captive market. And while contracts agreed at the time of privatisation would prevent road owners from denying access to residents, discriminatory pricing could have a similar effect. For example, a road owner seeking to obtain property adjoining his road or to take advantage of a captive market could charge prohibitive tolls (which for commercial reasons (see above) would not be applied to through traffic). But, once again, this should not be seen as justifying state price controls. Rather, the privatisation process would include contractual arrangements with regard to pricing in order to protect residents. It is also likely that rights of way for pedestrians, bicycles and horses would be preserved without charge, even though they would impose costs on road owners and motorists. Many major roads follow historic rights of way that pre-date motor vehicles (Highways Agency, n.d.).

Pricing technologies

Compared with the situation with motorways, the introduction of user charging on major roads is challenging. There may be long stretches of road, say in mountainous areas, which are suitable for conventional toll booths. In many locations there may also be convenient bottlenecks, such as bridges, where tolls can be charged. Most major roads, however – particularly those in urban areas – are characterised by numerous intersections with minor roads, which could easily be used to bypass toll collection points. Swiss-style 'vignettes' might be a suitable alternative on such routes so that users pay a fixed cost per annum, recognising the high fixed costs and low congestion on some parts of these systems. The ratio of revenues to administration costs is generally likely to be lower on many major roads than on motorways – given lower average traffic levels. This weakens the case for expensive, high-technology electronic schemes – unless road owners cooperate on the installation of a widespread GPS charging technology. Nevertheless, entrepreneurs would undoubtedly discover solutions to the charging problems associated with major roads, and their choice of tolling method could well depend on the particular characteristics of their infrastructure.

Minor rural roads

The privatisation of minor rural roads shares many of the

Box 5 **Private road associations**

In Sweden, about two-thirds of the road network is owned by around sixty thousand private road associations (PRAs) (Malmberg Calvo and Ivarsson, 2006). This infrastructure consists of routes that are very lightly used with negligible through traffic. Nevertheless, one in four trips in Sweden starts or ends on a private road. Members of each association are property owners along the private road, with shares determined according to the size of their property and the traffic they generate. Financial responsibility for the roads rests with the members, who must pay a fee to cover maintenance and other costs. Each PRA has an elected board and a set of bylaws. Many larger PRAs pay a fee to an umbrella organisation, the National Federation of Private Road Associations, which covers liability insurance, political representation and so on.

Sweden's Private Roads Act sets out how property owners can form PRAs and how these organisations should be constituted and operated (ibid.: 332). It also outlines how the costs of the roads should be distributed among the owners. In practice, a government surveyor determines this according to the rules of the Act. Private property owners wishing to set up a PRA can apply to the authorities, who will then appoint an impartial surveyor (ibid.). There is therefore a bespoke

challenges presented by major roads, in particular concerns over property access and rights of way. Accordingly, similar contractual solutions would apply. In addition, many minor roads are uneconomic in the sense that their maintenance costs (and the administration costs associated with user charging) exceed the legal framework for PRAs, which also ensures the collection of fees.

The PRAs manage the roads at less cost and with better results than the state road agencies (ibid.). Indeed, the cost is often less than half that of comparable government-managed roads. This reflects the improved incentive structures associated with private ownership and the time- and place-specific knowledge available to PRA members. Potholes, for example, are spotted and repaired quickly, before further expensive damage takes place, because, unlike state officials, the private owners face the full consequences of delaying action – including more expensive repair bills and damage to their vehicles.

The Swedish PRA system is not an entirely free market solution since many PRAs receive government grants to cover part of their costs and the roads remain subject to various state regulations and a tight legal framework. Accordingly, there are significant barriers to entrepreneurship and to owners' flexibility in introducing tolls, restricting access and determining rules. Nevertheless, PRAs demonstrate that private, community-level ownership is a practical option for denationalised minor roads and suggest that private ownership brings very substantial benefits in terms of economic efficiency.

tolls that could be received from the relatively small number of users. This greatly complicates the process of privatisation.

The privatisation process

Those minor roads that are economically viable could be privatised through the options discussed above, with contractual agreements on access and pricing for affected land owner. It is clearly objectionable for taxpayers to continue funding the maintenance of uneconomic roads, which are perhaps used by just a handful of motorists to access remote houses and farms. In such cases, the best option may be to give ownership of the roads to the owners of adjoining land, either individually or collectively. Individual ownership would be particularly suitable for sections of minor road serving a single property. Collective forms of ownership would guarantee by contract access rights to individual properties. The example of private road associations in Sweden demonstrates how community ownership can work (Box 5).

In some instances, depending on the nature of existing rights of way, the new owners would benefit from the opportunity to restrict access by non-residents, with large potential benefits for reducing crime and antisocial behaviour (for example, fly-tipping). Yet the roads would certainly also represent a considerable liability. Under many legal jurisdictions, road owners could be deemed liable for road accidents caused by poor maintenance of the infrastructure, even if the victims were trespassers.[6] Insurance costs could be significant. Owners might also be obliged to meet certain regulatory standards. And forms of collective ownership could potentially involve decision-making costs and legal disputes. For example, disputes could arise as to the kind of vehicles that would be allowed to use the road, given the implications for maintenance costs. The relevant 'constitution' of a

---

6   For example, in England and Wales, under the Occupiers' Liability Act 1984.

collective ownership structure would have to be drafted with care and with one eye to possible potential problems arising from the future development of new transport technologies. The development of standardised residential-road ownership contracts can be envisaged; a development that would reduce the economic cost of the privatisation process.

In summary, there would be substantial disincentives to take ownership of minor rural roads. These could, however, be mitigated by a change in the law on liability and by the removal of statutory road standards. Such measures could form part of the legislation facilitating road privatisation. A less desirable option than privatisation would be for local governments to simply stop maintaining uneconomic minor roads, which eventually would become too degraded for vehicles. Alternatively, ownership could be transferred to some kind of trust or to charitable organisations.

Pricing issues

The administration costs associated with pricing mean with most charging methods it would not generally be worthwhile charging users of minor rural roads. Pricing could be imposed at low marginal cost using satellite-based electronic charging schemes, but the incentives to install equipment could be poor for consumers who rarely used busy major roads or motorways. Their vehicles would have to be fitted with expensive tracking devices, their movements would be monitored, but they would receive no benefits in terms of reduced congestion or improved infrastructure (because such investment would remain uneconomic). The difficulties of pricing at the margin, however, do not mean that revenue could not be raised and charging not implemented.

Owners would have to determine their own subscription mechanisms for raising funds for repair, etc. In addition, the umbrella organisation of road owners could offer to potential users a periodic season ticket that allowed them to use all rural roads owned by affiliated bodies – this would be in addition to any access rights owners wish to offer.

Minor urban roads

The privatisation of minor urban roads differs from that of minor rural roads in several important ways. Firstly, the ratio of residents and users to road space is far higher, so their viability is more assured. Secondly, many residential roads do not constitute long-standing rights of way. Their purpose is merely to provide access to the adjoining properties. Finally, the benefits of privatisation are likely to be much greater in cities (where rates of crime and antisocial behaviour are generally much higher: see, for example, Higgins et al., 2010: 168) given the opportunities for owners to exclude undesirables from their streets, as well as to implement parking arrangements tailored to the specific preferences of residents. Many forms of antisocial behaviour, such as graffiti, fly-tipping, noise from car stereos and vandalism, could be significantly reduced with private residential roads. The Urban Street Associations of St Louis, Missouri, provide one model of how such roads could be administered (Box 6). In the UK the greater population density and smaller size of housing units would bring additional benefits from privatisation. For example, streets could become safe places for children to play again and residents could manage their own on-street parking arrangements, which are currently an enormous problem in many towns.

Box 6 **Urban street associations**

In St Louis, Missouri, there is a long history of streets being managed by 'street associations' composed of residents. Many associations date back to the nineteenth century with their rules set out in covenants attached to adjoining properties. In the 1970s, however, residents in many public streets petitioned the city authorities to transfer ownership to street associations in order to address growing problems with antisocial behaviour, through traffic and so on. About one thousand St Louis streets were 'privatised' in this way (Elliot, 1989).

The associations are responsible for road maintenance, street lighting, security, sewers and waste disposal. Moreover, some associations have restricted access to their streets by putting up chains and gates to deter criminals. Privatisation therefore enabled residents to create 'defensible space', which has been shown empirically to reduce crime (Newman, 1973). The street associations themselves may also help foster a sense of community and improve incentives for private action to prevent crime and antisocial behaviour. Newman (1981) found that crime rates were far lower in privately managed streets than in similar public streets. The private streets also stabilised the surrounding area, helping arrest urban decay, and also boasted significantly higher house prices. Clearly the privatisation of urban streets in itself is not a solution to all the problems associated with major social and demographic changes in cities. Nevertheless, the evidence from St Louis does suggest that private streets can mitigate significantly the negative effects on residents.

The privatisation process

The process of privatising minor urban roads would be straightforward with newly built infrastructure (see below). With established streets, residents could be given the 'right to own' by making a request to the relevant government authority (local councils in the case of the UK). This proposal would be similar to the successful 'right-to-buy' scheme for council house tenants (see King, 2010), although in this instance there would be no charge (since property developers paid for the construction of the roads and taxpayers for their maintenance). As with minor rural roads, there would, however, be considerable liabilities attached to ownership, and once again changes to the legal framework would help address these. Yet the benefits of privatisation could be expected to lead to higher property prices and lower insurance costs, in many cases tipping the incentives in favour of privatisation. To maximise the benefits, some planning liberalisation would be required. While this policy is beneficial in general (see Evans, 1988; Pennington, 2002), the installation of gates, walls and fences could be exempted from planning controls as an initial step in the right direction. Moreover, road-owning residents should ideally be given a proportionate discount on local taxes to reflect the savings accruing to local governments.

On some streets there may be few residents and enough space so that the road could be physically divided with boundaries in order to afford absolute ownership over the access routes to properties. In such instances this might well be the preferred option since it may reduce the possibility of future disputes with other owners. In other cases the question arises of whether privatisation should take place only in the event of the unanimous agreement of the owners of the properties along the street. If unanimity were not achieved then at least one owner would be forced into a transaction against his will, in apparent violation of liberal principles. At the same time, if the local authority continued to maintain the street using taxation this activity would also involve involuntary takings. An alternative option would be to treat the street as common property if unanimity could not be achieved. Yet, in this instance, there could be problems in the organisation of maintenance. There would be incentives for some individuals to free-ride on others who had a larger stake in keeping the road in good condition. On many residential streets 'selective incentives', such as the desire for good relations with one's neighbours, would probably ensure cooperation (see Olson, 1965). There would still be disadvantages compared with privatisation, however, since it could be more difficult to restrict access or engage in entrepreneurial activity. Over time, the comparative success of those streets that opted for privatisation would encourage more of the 'holdouts' to give way.

Once regulatory barriers had been removed, the privatisation of local roads would proceed by a process of evolution and emulation. The success of early adopters would encourage others to follow suit. Moreover, in the context of a liberal planning environment, existing neighbourhoods would be in competition with new neighbourhoods built by private developers where private roads formed part of the package sold to prospective residents and business occupiers (see Beito et al., 2004). Over time, areas with public roads would tend to decline as more people and firms moved to private streets in order to enjoy the various benefits. A higher and higher proportion of urban space would be privately owned. And private owners could speed up the process by purchasing properties on public streets and transferring those streets to private ownership, benefiting from the resulting uplift in values (particularly if the properties were derelict or abandoned through neighbourhood decline).

In a similar way, roads in town centres could be bought by businesses acting cooperatively. They could then determine a mix of charges that was regarded as appropriate given the level of congestion and the desire by businesses to attract business and customers to the town centre.

Pricing issues

As with minor rural roads, the high ratio of collection costs to potential toll revenues means that pricing is unlikely to be worthwhile on most minor urban roads. In some instances, however, residents/owners could profit by re-engineering their streets to create 'rat runs' for through traffic – for example, by reopening through-routes closed off by local governments. Where privatisation involves collective ownership structures, the 'constitution' of the organisation should set out the rules relevant for making such decisions and for charging.

New roads

New roads present few of the difficulties associated with the privatisation of existing state-owned roads. There are, however, some specific issues.

Planning controls

The first is the extent to which new road schemes would be subject to government planning controls, rather than being exempted and subject instead to private negotiation between road entrepreneurs and property owners. Given that land use changes in general are subject to planning controls, private roads would also be subject to the requirement to obtain consent. Unfortunately this means that politicians and officials could effectively direct transport policy, even though ownership of the new infrastructure remained nominally private. Many of the benefits of private ownership could be lost in this way. For example, road builders could be forced to install bus or cycle lanes or even pay money towards competing rail services in order to be granted planning permission. These kinds of deals (known as section 106 agreements, but now being reformed) are certainly commonplace in the UK planning system. Rather than locating new road schemes according to market demand, road entrepreneurs could be forced to consider 'social benefits' and could end up changing their plans significantly in order to gain bureaucratic approval. As is the case with the UK retail sector (Barclay, 2012), planners could even decide that existing capacity in a given area is already sufficient and that there is no need for additional road space – a policy with negative implications for competition in the roads sector. Nevertheless, even if existing planning controls persisted, it still seems likely that many new roads would be given permission. In some localities congestion problems are so severe that new infrastructure would be very welcome.

A separate issue is whether new motorways and major roads, which generally cross several local government boundaries, should face local planning controls or whether national legislation should apply. Negotiation of routes with several different local governments would clearly be costly and time-consuming.

When private companies built Britain's railways in the nineteenth century, they generally obtained permission through Parliamentary Acts, thereby bypassing local controls. And many countries today have special institutions charged with deciding or advising on infrastructure projects of national importance. (In England, the Planning Inspectorate examines proposed schemes and makes a recommendation to the relevant secretary of state.)

Compulsory purchase

Large infrastructure projects typically involve compulsory purchase (known as eminent domain in the USA). Land is confiscated from owners along the route, though compensation is paid. This is clearly objectionable when property rights are central to a free-market society. Fortunately there are several reasons to believe that compulsory purchase would not be necessary for the construction of private roads.

Clearly there is no need to 'confiscate' land to build roads across unowned wilderness areas. And in practice developed areas are typically characterised by existing routes that could be reused more productively as toll roads – for example, railways or canals (see Withrington, 2004). The notion that the absence of compulsory purchase would prevent the construction of new roads can be dismissed. It should also be noted that a combination of private ownership and road pricing would lead to more efficient use of existing capacity.

Nevertheless, there is also an argument that land must be obtained in order to build infrastructure that follows direct routes. A small number of holdouts could force road builders to make a large diversion if they refused to sell or lease their land. As Block

(1979: 218) has pointed out, it may be possible to build a tunnel under or a bridge over a holdout's property. This may, however, be prohibitively expensive for some projects. It is, though, easier to introduce diversions to roads than to railways and, to the extent to which alternative routes exist, holdout problems are reduced.

Of course, the notion of an efficient network is, to some extent, contingent on a static view of the spatial pattern of economic activity. In practice, economic geographies adapt to the available infrastructure, and new transport links in market economies will tend to attract both residential and business development, particularly in the absence of government planning controls. A system of private planning, in which a high proportion of individuals would be members of 'proprietary communities' (see Beito et al., 2004), would also help circumvent any conceivable disadvantages resulting from the absence of compulsory purchase, as voluntary rules on new transport infrastructure could be agreed contractually in advance.

It should be noted that, although the authors are not convinced that compulsory purchase will be necessary to build new roads, this is largely a separate issue from that of who owns the roads. Compulsory purchase was used in the context of the development of the private railway system in the nineteenth century. If compulsory purchase is retained, however, it should be reformed. Those selling land for the building of a new road should be able to obtain the fair market value of the land in its new use as a road – possibly enhanced further by the prospect of housing and business development close to the road.

Financing new roads

Since new roads would no longer be funded through taxation,

Box 7 **The M6 Toll**

The M6 Toll is the only example of a privately funded toll motorway in the UK. Completed in 2003, it provides an alternative route to a congested section of the original M6 which passes through Birmingham. A private company, Midland Expressway Ltd (MEL), won the 53-year concession to build and operate the road. Construction and operation were carried out without government subsidies or guarantees with costs covered by revenues from unregulated tolls.

Although the M6 Toll shows that private toll motorways are a practical proposition, even in heavily regulated Britain, both traffic levels and financial returns have been disappointing, with the project making small losses in the first few years of operation. This largely reflects the high financing costs of the project, which resulted from the political/planning risks involved (for example, the real possibility that politicians would cancel the scheme, change the contract and so on).*

The inflated financing cost associated with political risk is just one way in which the M6 Toll departed from the free-

they would depend on private-sector investment. There are numerous examples of privately funded toll roads operating successfully around the world, even in the UK (see Box 7).

It is therefore worth setting out various financing options and examining the financial viability of projects. The details will, of course, vary according to the type of road.

Take the example of a new 100-mile rural motorway constructed in the UK, one of the most expensive countries in the world for building new infrastructure. The construction market development of private roads. Importantly, the route also faces unfair competition from the existing M6, which is free at the point of use, reducing the incentive to use the M6 Toll except at congested peak times. Furthermore, strict planning controls restrict the ability of the motorway owners to profit from land development along the route. Finally, the fiscal framework means that users must pay fuel duty and vehicles excise duty as well as the toll.

The M6 Toll provides important lessons on the institutional arrangements that would be conducive to the successful financing, construction and operation of private trunk roads and motorways. In particular, it suggests that competing routes should be privatised simultaneously to avoid 'crowding out' by state-owned infrastructure – or, as a minimum, incorporate some method of marginal pricing – and that privatisation should be accompanied by significant reductions in motoring taxation to limit fiscal distortions to the transport market.

* For more details, see Wellings and Lipson (2008: 24–5).

cost is estimated at £3 billion, including the pricing infrastructure.[7] In fact, there are good economic reasons to believe that the private road entrepreneurs would be able to dramatically reduce the costs of construction. An attractive gross yield of 8 per cent would require annual toll revenues of £240 million. If the route

7   Archer and Glaister (2006) provide an estimate of the average cost of building a six-lane motorway at £6.46 million per km (c. £10 million per mile) in 2003 prices (based on Starkie, 2002). This figure has been adjusted upwards according to increases in the road construction tender price index with an allowance for the costs of installing charging infrastructure, etc.

matched the national motorway average traffic level of around 80,000 vehicles per day (DfT, 2011b) – and unlike governments, entrepreneurs would be incentivised to build routes where they would attract traffic – an average charge of 8p per mile would be sufficient. Assuming higher charges for goods vehicles, which make up a significant proportion of motorway traffic, tolls for cars could be as little as 6p per mile, or £6 for the whole route. For most cars, this would be less than the fuel duty alone paid for a journey of this length. In comparison with current government roads, users would benefit from lower congestion costs and faster speeds, and would also gain from lower wear and tear and insurance costs (see below) – suggesting motorists may also be willing to pay higher charges to use more efficient private roads and that some projects could still be viable even with high rates of fuel duty.

Moreover, there would be several sources of profits apart from toll revenues. Road owners could develop land along the route, capturing the rise in values resulting from the new infrastructure (see Harrison, 2006). Even if they did not own nearby land, they could auction the locations of junctions to the highest bidders. It is not inconceivable that, in some areas, the development of surrounding land could finance the entire costs of constructing major new roads. Indeed, with regard to minor roads this already happens in the case of new private housing developments in many countries (including the UK). On their completion, ownership of the roads is typically signed over to local government. In these cases, ownership could instead be transferred from developers to residents, who would manage the streets through an association, as discussed above. Indeed, private roads could be part of a package of services provided outside the state, as seen in numerous 'proprietary communities' across the world (Box 8).

Further subsidiary sources of revenue for new roads might include leasing services along the route (hotels, food, petrol stations and so on); advertising hoardings; and Internet/mobile phone facilities and so on. Thus there should be no particular difficulties financing new road projects with attractive rates of return. Entrepreneurs could finance schemes through share issues or bank loans, for example. It should be noted, however, that investors would demand a risk premium if there were a significant possibility of political interference in the development of new roads – for example, if a government sought to regulate tolls or exempt certain types of user. As in the energy industry, an unstable regulatory or ownership framework could seriously choke off investment.

The fiscal framework

The economic viability of private roads will be affected significantly by the fiscal framework within which owners operate. Motoring taxes, such as special fuel and vehicle taxes, may reduce returns to private operators by reducing total consumer demand and absorbing spending that might otherwise be devoted to tolls. To the extent that tax rates on road users affect toll revenues, they may also introduce an element of political risk into the calculation of expected returns from new investment.

Some of the justifications for special road-user taxes disappear once ownership of the infrastructure is transferred to the private sector. The argument that the taxes are needed to fund construction and maintenance is certainly no longer valid. Accident costs

Box 8 **Private roads and private communities**
Across the world, particularly outside Europe, private
communities with private roads are proving attractive
to residents and businesses seeking an alternative to
government-managed space. Such communities provide a
range of services (roads, street lighting, sewerage, security
and so on) and typically have their own rules determining the
use of properties, access to the roads, acceptable behaviour
and so on (see Beito et al., 2004). In some instances,
residents' associations are responsible for management and
they will typically have their own constitutions to guide
decision-making. An alternative is the 'hotel' model, in which
private owners determine the rules and residents enter into
a contract to observe them. In practice, a wide range of
institutional models is possible. The key advantage is that
new communities must market themselves to prospective
residents. In this way, a market discovery process is set
in train, and rules and institutions can be adapted to suit
individual preferences. Community rules can therefore be
far more nuanced than under the one-size-fits-all approach
typical of local government. For example, an environmentalist
community would be free to ban cars, mandate that all
homes were carbon neutral and source all its energy from
renewable sources.
   Despite their advantages, the development of private

are paid by users through insurance and/or personal losses.[8] Local
environmental costs such as noise and some types of air pollution

---

8 Even the healthcare costs of accidents can be reclaimed by government from insurers through the Injury Costs Recovery scheme.

communities has been hampered by government intervention. In many locations, they may face opposition from town planners and politicians, who fear greater social fragmentation. Moreover, residents generally have to pay for local services twice – as well as community fees they must also pay local taxes (even though their use of local-government-supplied services may be limited). Nevertheless, the rapid growth of private communities in many countries suggests that the benefits outweigh the additional costs. Security is often a key consideration, as shown by the popularity of gated settlements in high-crime countries such as South Africa and Brazil (see Landman and Schonteich, 2002). Private developments with restricted access and armed security at entry points may be the size of small towns and include offices, hospitals, schools and shopping centres as well as homes (for example, Alphaville in São Paulo). Private ownership of the roads is clearly essential in addressing fears of crime. Indeed, in crime-plagued Johannesburg there are hundreds of examples of local residents taking the initiative by blocking off public roads and restricting access without the permission of the local authority (Landman, 2003: 26).

The approach to both financing and governance of such communities demonstrates that such road systems are, in fact, club goods and not public goods, as is often supposed.

can be dealt with via free land markets and do not require any fiscal intervention (if planning regulations prevent land markets from internalising these effects then the resulting 'negative exter-nalities' are the result of government intervention, not the actions of road users or owners; Wellings, 2006a). This leaves larger-scale environmental impacts, in particular the hypothesised effect of carbon emissions on the global climate. But given scientific uncertainty and severe knowledge limitations, it is far from clear that anthropogenic emissions are significantly changing the climate; that the costs of any projected climate change exceed the benefits; and that the benefits of policies to mitigate climate change will exceed the associated costs. In any case, even rather high estimates of the 'social costs' of carbon emissions (for example, Stern, 2006) imply taxes on road fuel that are a small fraction of the current levies imposed in western Europe. A carbon tax applied equally to all sectors of the economy would probably not represent an existential threat to the private roads industry, particularly if it replaced the motoring taxes currently imposed.[9]

In conclusion, road users should not be the subject of special taxes. Private ownership of the infrastructure completely undermines any rationale for such levies. Indeed, the transport sector should be on a level playing field with other economic activities in order to maximise allocative efficiency. This also means public transport would no longer benefit from grants, subsidies and tax exemptions.

Changing the rules of the road

Government roads are subject to a wide range of regulations covering driver behaviour, signposts, the characteristics of vehicles, insurance, speed limits and so on. The privatisation of roads raises the question of whether states should continue

---

9   Such a tax would be applied to public transport as well as electricity and domestic heating – perhaps making it harder for politicians to increase its rate arbitrarily.

to impose such rules. Various arguments could be deployed in defence of continued government regulation. First, there is an efficiency argument. If certain standards and practices are adopted across the network this avoids the problem of drivers having to adhere to different rules every time they move on to a road controlled by a different owner. Extreme examples would be if different owners made different rules about which side of the road one should drive on or changed the colours used for stop and go in traffic lights. One can imagine the chaos that might result. It is also contended that regulation can help businesses since it saves them the costs associated with developing rules themselves. There are clearly also safety implications from the absence of standardised guidelines. Advocates of regulation typically point to the 'social costs' of unregulated behaviour, such as the health costs of accidents that are borne by general taxpayers.

It is quite wrong, however, to assume that the removal of government regulations would lead to a completely unregulated environment for private roads. Owners would have strong economic incentives to introduce rules that promoted safety and the efficient flow of traffic. The belief that state action is required to standardise certain practices is also erroneous. Rules and standards can arise spontaneously through the free actions of individuals and businesses, as seen in the recent evolution of the Internet. And for reasons of safety and efficiency, private road owners would almost certainly adopt established practice on matters such as common signage, traffic signals, road markings and so on. But, unlike governments, private operators would have strong incentives to change non-essential rules if it presented opportunities to reduce costs or increase revenue. Indeed, subjecting road regulations to the market discovery process promises to deliver significant economic gains. Road owners would be free to try out various innovations that they hoped would attract more business to their routes. They would be rewarded for successful ideas by improved profits. In contrast to the situation with state-controlled roads, only those changes satisfying consumer preferences would survive in the long term. Several of the most important regulatory issues are discussed below.

Speed limits

Under a private system there would be no national speed limits; the decision on the speeds that should be allowed would rest with the proprietors. Accordingly, where traffic levels and road conditions allowed, there could be dramatic increases in speed limits, or even no speed limits, as on some German autobahns, resulting in substantial reductions in travel times, with concomitant economic benefits (such as increased labour mobility). For example, with a speed limit of 100 miles per hour it would be theoretically possible to travel door to door from London to Manchester in just two hours, a significant improvement on current travel times (even by rail or air). Moreover, the introduction of high-speed coaches on uncongested toll motorways clearly has the potential to revolutionise low-cost intercity travel.[10] Highly subsidised, capital-intensive railways could be paved over to make way for dedicated busways (see Withrington, 2004).

Several options would enable road owners to increase speed while improving safety, such as widening lanes; limiting slow-moving vehicles to the inside lane; removing roadside obstacles

---

10   Coaches are currently limited to 100 km/h as the result of EU legislation.

such as trees; increasing the separation between carriageways; installing an advanced hazard warning system; and creating a separation zone between the lanes and the hard shoulder. There will be other techniques which will emerge in a competitive market. The point here is not to prescribe practices but rather to demonstrate the practicality of constructing or adapting roads for high speed. The commercial decision to develop high-speed routes would depend on whether the entrepreneur considered that high-speed facilities would attract sufficient customers to return a profit and whether the potential benefits would outweigh the possible costs, such as any impact on accident rates.

Goods vehicles

There would be no statutory limit on the size or weight of goods vehicles using private roads. On some routes it might prove profitable for owners to develop infrastructure for very large trucks, perhaps between major ports and major cities, steelworks and coal-fired power stations. Vehicles could be scaled up, thereby reducing the unit labour cost of road transport. 'Road trains' – such as those used in Australia – could be deployed, should road owners decide to facilitate this. Other road owners may prefer much more onerous restrictions – or may wish to restrict heavy good vehicle use at particular times such as on bank holidays. Road privatisation and deregulation would present opportunities for very substantial productivity improvements in the haulage sector, with, *ceteris paribus*, a resulting lowering of transport costs for businesses.

Insurance

Insurance for damage to third parties is generally compulsory on state-owned roads. Indeed, for many road users insurance is the largest single component of their transport costs (AA, 2011). But in a deregulated environment, private road owners might not require drivers to purchase insurance, since lower motoring costs could increase traffic and toll revenues. One option would be to bundle insurance as part of the road toll. Alternatively drivers could be left to decide for themselves whether to buy cover.

It should be noted that even if compulsory insurance laws remained in place, the privatisation of roads could significantly reduce insurance costs. This is because road owners would have strong incentives to lower accident rates. Accidents would disrupt traffic flow and reduce toll revenues. They could also damage profits through the effects on a road's reputation for safety. Under some legal frameworks, owners might also have to pay substantial compensation to victims if it were shown they were somehow at fault. Private owners would also have more freedom to address threats to safety, for example by excluding unsafe drivers and vehicles. More flexibility in the setting of speed limits and other rules of the road would enable better tailoring to local conditions. To protect children, private residential streets might have speed limits of 10 mph or less, as found already in many privately owned communities. Owners of rural roads could ban overtaking (the main cause of serious accidents) while at the same time limiting their use by slow-moving vehicles. These are just possibilities. In practice a market discovery process would encourage all manner of innovations in safety, together with efficient trade-offs between safety and other considerations such as infrastructure costs and vehicle speed.

Vehicle standards

Private road owners could also decide the characteristics of the vehicles allowed to use their infrastructure. Government-imposed vehicle standards, particularly relating to safety and exhaust emissions, significantly increase the costs of road use. As with insurance, it may be in road owners' interest to remove artificial constraints on the consumption of their services. At the same time, any relaxation of vehicle standards would have to be balanced against the resulting effects on safety and harm imposed on adjoining property owners. Importantly, such private regulation would be subject to rational economic calculation rather than arbitrary political will. And, as with speed, weight limits and insurance, private control has the potential to deliver very substantial economic gains.

4 THE POLITICAL ECONOMY OF PRIVATISATION

Although the economic case for denationalising roads is strong, there are numerous political barriers to privatisation in the form of incentive structures associated with state ownership. A range of interest groups exert significant influence on roads policy. They include government finance ministries, transport bureaucracies and environmental NGOs (Rawcliffe, 1995; Dudley and Richardson, 2003; Wellings, 2006b). This chapter concludes by examining the political economy of road privatisation.

The following discussion considers the incentives facing different interest groups in a potential privatisation process. A denationalisation of the roads sector would impact upon interests ranging from local residents to taxpayers, from road safety campaigners to environmentalists and from bureaucrats to politicians, to name but a few. The analysis focuses on those likely to have a decisive influence on the privatisation process. What are their interests and what do they stand to gain from a private road market rather than administration and ownership by the state?

Finance ministries

Government finance ministries are central to the development of transport policy around the world, although the precise mix of national, regional and local control varies.[1] These bureaucracies typically set tax rates for road users and also determine levels of expenditure on road networks (see Newbery, 1998: 2).

In many countries, special road-user taxes represent a significant source of tax revenues. For example, in the UK they raised approximately £35 billion in 2011.[2] As noted in Chapter 3, such taxes severely distort the transport market. Their continuation would threaten the development of an efficient market in private roads, particularly where high rates were imposed. But phasing out the taxation of road fuel would present a major difficulty for governments. They would either have to make spending cuts or raise taxes elsewhere to make up the resulting funding shortfall. Accordingly, they have the potential to be powerful opponents of such a policy.

Yet opposition by finance ministries to road privatisation would be short-sighted. Firstly, there is the possibility of considerable receipts from the sale of motorways and major roads. The strategic roads network in the UK, for example, has been valued at approximately £100 billion (see Mulheirn and Furness, 2010: 15) – and this could be a significant underestimate given the magnitude of road-user revenues and the relatively low-risk nature of the investment (see below). Receipts from a phased privatisation process could be used to fund reductions in road-user taxes. Indeed, a cast-iron commitment to use the receipts in this way would increase the amount raised since it would tend to raise toll revenues. Secondly, tax reductions could be further offset by reductions in government expenditure on roads – as

---

1   See, for example, Dudley and Richardson (2003).

2   Compared with less than £10 billion spent on the roads, much of it on anti-car traffic calming schemes, priority measures for buses and cyclists and so on (see Wellings, 2011).

investment and maintenance are transferred to the private sector. A third consideration is the strong likelihood that new technologies such as electric vehicles will start eating into fuel tax receipts in any case, thus reducing the disincentive to reform the existing fiscal framework. Finally, there will be a considerable long-term economic dividend from private ownership. Lower congestion, fewer accidents and faster journey times would increase productivity, leading to higher incomes and larger overall tax revenues. As awareness of the dynamic benefits of denationalising roads increases among treasury officials, they may well become more receptive to the policy. Indeed, if it were part of a general liberalisation of the transport sector, the fiscal benefits would be still greater, since public transport subsidies could be phased out.

Transport bureaucracies

The state ownership of roads is associated with vast transport bureaucracies. For example, in Britain the Department for Transport oversees the sector and undertakes high-level policy development and strategic planning; a subsidiary, the Highways Agency, is responsible for the construction, maintenance and management of the vast majority of motorways and trunk roads in England; local and/or regional authorities are responsible for the bulk of the road network (DfT, 2012a). Various national-level agencies enforce regulations. Supranational institutions, such as the European Commission, also play both a strategic and a regulatory role. The different tiers of governance employ several thousand officials.[3] Institutional arrangements are broadly similar

---

3   In England, the Highways Agency alone employs approximately four thousand staff (http://www.highways.gov.uk/aboutus/documents/

in other countries, although the role of 'regional' bodies (such as the states in the USA) may be significantly larger.

The denationalisation of roads implies the abolition of transport bureaucracies and even some sort of compromise model might involve their shrinkage to a regulatory oversight role (see Newbery, 1998). Accordingly, such agencies are likely to represent a significant obstacle to the process. In the case of previous privatisations, senior officials have succeeded in retaining a high degree of control (and, indeed, high-status, well-paid employment) through the imposition of complex regulatory frameworks on nominally privately owned industries. In this way, many of the benefits of privatisation have been lost.[4]

It is hard to see how the interests of transport bureaucrats can be reconciled with a genuine process of denationalisation in which regulatory controls are dismantled. The new private road owners would, of course, require technical expertise to manage and maintain their assets. Accordingly, some officials might expect to be re-employed in the private sector; and others might draw on their knowledge to become road entrepreneurs. To the extent that much bureaucratic activity would not be replicated in the private sector, however, and that bureaucrats lack the 'commercial mindedness' (Mises, 1935) to be successful in business, it seems highly likely that denationalisation would threaten the status and salaries of a high proportion of transport officials across all tiers of government. Given the demonstrable ability of senior officials to

---

CRS_632573_HA_Organisational_Structure_Annex.pdf). It is harder in practice to identify the number of civil servants specifically allocated to roads at the core Department for Transport, since they often have cross-modal thematic briefs.

4   The privatisation of British Rail is arguably the best-known example (see Hibbs et al., 2006).

influence policy,[5] this is a serious problem for any programme of road privatisation and suggests such a process will require considerable political commitment by its proponents.

Environmentalists

The environmental movement has exerted huge influence on the road policies of Western governments in recent decades. Despite growing traffic levels and congestion, policymakers have focused spending on public transport, in an attempt to fulfil 'sustainability' targets and address climate change (for example, DETR, 1998). Road users have also been subject to increasing environmental regulation, for example through the imposition of tighter emissions standards. Fuel duties have risen dramatically and car prices reflect ever more stringent regulatory controls.

Environmentalists have tended to assume that extensive state intervention is required to minimise the negative external effects of road use on the environment. Notwithstanding the ecological disasters of the Soviet bloc, private enterprise is seen as putting profit above environmental protection. There is now a large body of evidence, however, that the main problem with environmental pollution is not the profit motive but rather the absence of enforceable property rights (Anderson and Leal, 2001: 149–51, 165–9; Beckerman, 2003: 52–6; Lomborg, 2001: 107, 113). Strong private property rights are the best protection against negative environmental impacts, and road privatisation clearly represents an extension of property rights in the transport sector. Private road builders, for example, would have to consider the effects of

---

5   In relation to transport policy in particular; see, for example, Dudley and Richardson (2003) and Wellings (2006b).

their activities on adjoining property owners, in terms of noise, air pollution and so on. Indeed, to minimise transaction costs, there will be strong incentives for the development within road markets of standardised procedures to decide compensation for damage to property.

Moreover, roads that are free at the point of use (or indeed flat-rate annual tolls) do not incentivise driving behaviour that minimises pollution. Charging based on usage induces a different traffic pattern. A road network that allocates traffic more efficiently reduces traffic jams, detours and unnecessary journeys that would otherwise have increased environmental pollution.

Motorists

Motorists have tended to have little influence over transport policy in recent decades. This observation is consistent with public choice theory since they are a dispersed group with poor incentives for individual members to engage in collective action (see Olson, 1965). Accordingly, more concentrated groups such as the haulage industry and farmers have been far more active in campaigning against road policies, as seen, for example, in the UK fuel protests of 2000. Motoring groups such as the Automobile Association had considerable input into policy in the early twentieth century, but this declined as the membership expanded and its interests became less focused (Plowden, 1971). Nevertheless, policymakers may factor in the views of motorists to the extent that their views affect voting patterns, although clearly transport policies are just a small part of the packages offered by political parties to voters during elections.

Many motorists fear that the introduction of road pricing,

whether or not part of a privatisation, will increase their travel costs, since taxes such as fuel duty will remain while additional road charges are also imposed. Indeed, opinion surveys suggest that support for road pricing increases markedly if new charges are matched by reductions in fuel duty and other motoring taxes (see RAC Foundation, 2006). The privatisation process should therefore include proportionate reductions in road-user taxation in order to address the objections of payers of road-user taxes (as well as for the economic reasons already discussed). Ideally, distortionary taxes should be phased out altogether.

The incentives facing drivers vary according to their individual usage patterns. Depending on the tax framework, drivers with low usage may be cross-subsidising the road network (for example, through fixed taxes on vehicles). In a privatised system, they would generally pay for their usage only – if they don't use the roads, they cannot be charged.[6] This would appear to create strong incentives for low-mileage users – such as pensioners – to support privatisation. Furthermore, a roads market would result in administrative efficiency gains and therefore lower costs, so even drivers with a high usage profile are likely to end up paying less than they do today. They will also arrive faster, enjoying a safer and less stressful journey. Motorists would therefore be major beneficiaries from the move to a private road industry. Their concerns about the introduction of road pricing are understandable, however, given the history of motoring taxation.

---

6   This may not be entirely true with some roads that are little used and to which access might be controlled using some kind of subscription basis.

Residents

There are numerous examples of local residents' groups opposing the construction of new infrastructure and even influencing transport policies at national level (see, for example, Bryant, 1995). The benefits of new road schemes are likely to be dispersed while the environmental costs are concentrated on the properties directly adjacent to the route. The incentives for local residents to engage in collective action are therefore very strong, and personal relationships between neighbours and within communities can act as a deterrent to free-riding.

The perspective of residents has already been discussed with regard to externalities. Though negative externalities, such as air pollution and noise, are most commonly raised, positive network externalities often seem to be taken for granted and are mostly unnoticed. It was concluded above that rational road operators, users and residents or their representatives would enter into negotiations. Whereas the residents would most likely claim compensation for the negative externalities they are exposed to, in turn they might be asked to pay for the positive externalities they enjoy owing to the presence of the road network. For example, a residents' association might be asked to contribute towards a new motorway that improved accessibility and boosted local property values. Although there are transaction costs involved in a negotiation process, these are not sufficient to require state action. Institutions such as private associations, clubs or other groups of residents, users, owners or operators help minimise transaction costs. As a result, such externalities are considered in the stakeholders' utility functions, whether during the construction of new roads, purchase of existing roads, usage or residence along the road. In a private road market, residents, users and operators are in charge. In a state road administration, however, bureaucrats may focus on their own utility functions owing to a legal monopoly of law creation and enforcement.

Assuming that local residents nonetheless prefer to maximise their own utility, they will benefit from private road operations. Not only will they finally be able to negotiate for compensation for harmful externalities, such external effects are also expected to be less of a nuisance in a private road industry. Efficient road management, for example by congestion or peak-load pricing, will reduce traffic jams and corresponding levels of air pollution. In contrast to the situation with state roads, entrepreneurs have an inherent interest in their roads being run well and customers not defecting to inter-modal competitors or other roads owing to long delays on their networks.

Prices of properties close to road schemes may increase to reflect future compensation revenues and the negotiating powers of property owners. Also, residents may run their own road operations and participate in the decision-making processes with regard to their local environment and road infrastructure. They may decide to operate their local neighbourhood roads, imposing limited access rights and thus increasing child safety, reducing congestion, noise and even crime. Alternatively, they may ask their local road company to provide for limited access only. Associated services such as cleaning, gardening and security could also be provided as part of the package. Local residents would be better off with a market in roads owing to the choice and decision-making and negotiating power the market conveys on all stakeholders, rather than on a small group of government road planners.

Politicians

Politicians supporting the denationalisation of roads can expect to benefit electorally as the advantages of the policy become clear. In the short term, receipts from privatisation would enable politicians to make deep cuts to unpopular taxes such as fuel duties. In the long term, the significant economic benefits deriving from the policy – including faster travel times and much lower congestion – will lead to higher living standards and the prospect of further cuts in tax rates as overall tax revenues increase as a result of efficiency gains. Politicians may also be able to claim credit for much lower accident rates on the roads and increased mobility of labour (and therefore lower unemployment).

The advantages of privatisation for local politicians may be particularly significant. The transfer of residential roads to individuals and community organisations promises to ameliorate many local problems such as crime, antisocial behaviour and unsuitable parking arrangements. Many of these problems have proved persistent and difficult to solve by other means. Road privatisation offers a low-cost solution and promises considerable benefits for local politicians that support the policy.

Finally, the politics of roads should be considered in the context of the current economic problems facing many Western countries. In the medium term, a privatisation programme could raise funds and reduce government debt and government spending. In addition, the expected productivity gains resulting from privatisation could make a major contribution to growth and recovery.

Opposition to private roads: a response

Innovations and other disruptions to markets usually provoke reactions from current market players or stakeholders to defend their position. Lobbying government for special laws, regulations and subsidies that will only distort the market further can be an effective strategy. Protectionism, in various forms, is widely deployed across what are often deemed market economies. Francis gives a particularly telling example of how innovators were discredited with respect to railways that required parliamentary approval in order to start operations:

> Next to the canal owner, the most important opposition was naturally expected from the landholder, and by both interests every art was used to produce an effectual hindrance. Every report which could promote a prejudice, every rumour which could affect a principle, was spread. The country gentleman was told that the smoke would kill the birds as they passed over the locomotive. The public were informed that the weight of the engine would prevent its moving; and the manufacturer was told that the sparks from its chimney would burn his goods. The passenger was frightened by the assertion that life and limb would be endangered. Elderly gentlemen were tortured with the notion that they would be run over. Ladies were alarmed at the thought that their horses would take fright. Foxes and pheasants were to cease in the neighbourhood of a railway. Farmers were possessed with the idea that oats and hay would no more be marketable produce; horses would start and throw their riders, cows even, it was said, would cease to yield their milk in the neighbourhood of one of these infernal machines. (Francis, 1851: 101–2)

Even though lobbyists may not necessarily succeed in implementing a legal monopoly, positive discrimination in the form of temporary protections, licensing regimes, regulations, minimum prices, subsidies, etc., are worthwhile prizes to be attained instead.[7] In economics, such behaviour is referred to as rent-seeking:

> The government can, for example, help create, increase, or protect a group's monopoly position. In so doing, the government increases the monopoly rents of the favored groups, at the expense of the buyers of the group's products or services. The monopoly rents that the government can help provide are a prize worth pursuing, and the pursuit of these rents has been given the name of rent seeking. (Mueller, 1996: 229)

It is natural that opposition will arise against private roads. Most of that opposition, however, can be turned in favour of private roads once the benefits to various stakeholders – such as taxpayers, residents and politicians – become more widely understood. And while various special interest groups may continue to reject privatisation outright, others will welcome it, explore the entrepreneurial potential of a transport market and see benefits from both competition and cooperation. Nevertheless, the strength of opposition should not be underestimated. In the same way as railway entrepreneurs were discredited, objectors to private roads may argue that the environment will be harmed, drivers would have to pay more, the sector would face huge job losses and social instability would be encouraged – and on top of all this, it would be argued that safety and network integrity would be compromised. Defending their current interests,

---

7   In his article on occupational licensing, Friedman (2002: 137–60) explores the many excesses of government interventionism to restrict and regulate entrepreneurial activities.

rent-seekers will not hesitate to invent apocalyptic scenarios.

Notwithstanding potential – predominantly rent-seeking – opposition, we urge decision-makers to consider the benefits private road networks will bring to the economy. An efficient transport infrastructure is a distinct advantage for trade and industry and a decisive factor in companies' investment decisions when locating business or extending production capabilities.

Private road networks relieve the state budget of capital intensive investments for new roads and maintenance and refocus the state on its core tasks. Moreover, voter-taxpayers will appreciate lower taxes, whereas voter-drivers will appreciate shorter commuting or journey times and lower-cost fuel. Rather than paying flat fees on road usage, drivers can plan their journeys according to their preferences and will be charged for the roads they actually use – not for the ones they do not, as happens in the current tax regime.

This study has set out how a market for roads might be introduced, advocating denationalisation of existing roads and private provision of all new road infrastructure. Diversions from the consistent approach suggested here risk creating a hybrid or compromise that is inferior to the current situation. Dismantling the public road system and starting afresh is the only means to reap all cost advantages to the economy, individual consumers and voters. As such, the market – and thus individual preferences – should become central to the roads sector, displacing the centralised road bureaucracies that have held sway for far too long.

Policy recommendations

The political and economic implications of the above analysis are clear. Governments should adopt policies to denationalise existing roads and phase out fiscal and regulatory distortions in the transport sector. Although a private road market should be allowed to develop its own institutions and structures, there is a series of steps that must be taken by policymakers to move from the current state-dominated system to a market-based framework. These steps must be implemented in a context where several interest groups threaten to undermine the reforms. Key elements of the process are summarised below:

- Levies such as fuel duty and Vehicle Excise Duty in the UK undermine support for road pricing (and therefore privatisation) among key user groups as well as distorting transport markets. Such levies lose their rationale if privatisation takes place. Special taxes applied to the road sector but not to other transport modes or other sectors of the economy should therefore be phased out. Indeed, the combination of discriminatory tax treatment and state subsidies for public transport would represent unfair competition to owners of private roads. Specifically, the following should be done:
  - Fuel duty should be reduced from 60 pence a litre to 15 pence a litre. The authors believe that the duty should be abolished altogether, but it is assumed here that an element of duty would remain to reflect environmental costs of climate change (see above). While we are sceptical about the need for such taxes, that is an issue separate from that of the ownership of the roads and it is better –

not least for political reasons – not to confuse the issues. This measure would reduce fuel duty revenue by about £25 billion in 2015 (including the VAT charged on the duty), under the simplifying assumption that no increase in demand for fuel would arise from the lower price.

– Vehicle excise duty will raise about £6 billion in 2015. This should be abolished upon road privatisation.

• The reform of transport taxation could be part-funded by transfer of new road construction to the private sector, thereby reducing government spending on the road network. New infrastructure could be funded by tolls and other pricing mechanisms, property development or some combination of the two. Subsidies to public transport would also be phased out. Government spending on transport (including that by devolved bodies) is forecast to total approximately £20 billion, of which about £12 billion will be spent on public transport. In addition, VAT on public transport fares would net the Treasury about £2 billion per year (see Wellings, 2011).

• The privatisation of the network of major roads alone could yield about £150 billion if there were the cuts in motoring taxes proposed here and pricing introduced on the privatised road system.[8] Inefficient taxes would thereby be replaced by an efficient system of road tolls.

---

8   Maintenance costs based on DfT (2011b) and Highways Agency (2012); toll collection costs estimated at 6 per cent of revenues, based on the M6 Toll, which uses a variety of charging methods (MIG, 2006); indicative revenues from DfT (2011b); indicative market valuation based on sample of existing privately operated toll roads (Samuel, 2009). This estimate takes no account of changes in demand due to market pricing (which are subject to a high degree of uncertainty) or other sources of revenue (such as land development) and therefore should be viewed as indicative.

- Further revenue from privatisation could arise from the sale of roads that are not currently classed as trunk roads but which have most of the characteristics of trunk roads and which could be gradually privatised – this would include ring roads. Additional revenue would also arise from the privatisation of roads owned by local authorities that were sold to businesses or local residents.

- Local taxation should be reformed so that residents and voluntary associations providing services currently undertaken by local government do not effectively pay twice. Private roads reduce the maintenance burden on local authorities and their owners should accordingly receive a proportionate discount on local taxes. There is a strong case for exempting residents and businesses in proprietary communities from local taxes when local services, including roads, are provided privately.

- The long-term success of such a privatisation process could be undermined if governments determined the structure of the private roads industry in advance. Instead the market structure should be allowed to evolve through mergers and demergers which reflect commercial consdierations such as economies of scale and transaction costs.

- Price controls should not be imposed on private road owners. Such regulation would politicise the sector, discourage new investment and undermine competition. It could also reduce flotation receipts significantly. Concerns about monopoly power can best be addressed by removing artificial barriers to entry, both in the roads market and in transport and communication markets more generally.

- The full benefits of privatisation will also not be forthcoming if strict spatial planning controls remain in place. Planning regulations would enable government officials to direct the roads sector by the back door. Moreover, such a framework could severely hamper competition by erecting barriers to entry. The implications for private road networks developed as part of proprietary communities are particularly serious. Ideally, the denationalisation of roads should therefore be accompanied by a radical liberalisation of planning systems, with private planning taking a dominant role (see Pennington, 2002).

- Similarly, the externalities associated with road use should be addressed, where possible, by private negotiation between affected parties. The imposition of environmental levies by governments based on existing 'social cost' estimates,[9] although undesirable in many ways, would hamper but not completely undermine the privatisation process.

- Government regulations applied to roads and road users should not be applied to private roads. Instead, owners should be free to determine their own 'rules of the road', which accordingly are likely to be more precisely tailored to local conditions and consumer preferences. This also applies to the deployment of pricing technologies, where it is best to allow private road markets to develop standard practices. The retention of current regulations would suffocate entrepreneurial innovation and prevent very substantial efficiency gains.

- Local residents, individually where appropriate, but more

---

9   The Stern Review (Stern, 2006) suggested that the 'social cost' of carbon could be around $85/tCO2 (in 2000 prices), which would equate to approximately 15 pence per litre of petrol in 2015.

typically in voluntary associations, should be given the 'right to own' the residential roads adjoining their properties. A simple transfer process should be introduced, similar to the UK's 'right-to-buy' programme for social housing. This may involve reforming the law on rights of way so that private owners can control access to their roads. Newly constructed residential roads should no longer be adopted by local government but should be managed and maintained by private owners. There are many benefits to this, but one particular benefit would be the possibility of tradable residential parking spaces in densely populated towns with few garages.[10] While these sorts of benefits may seem minor it is, in fact, such local environmental issues which affect people's day-to-day lives to a much greater degree than the strategic issues with which governments like to concern themselves.

State control of road networks can be rolled back. Case studies from around the world demonstrate that ownership by private bodies is highly successful given the right institutional framework. The rewards in terms of increased economic efficiency and improved safety promise to be substantial. It just remains for policymakers to face down vested interests and free the roads from the dead hand of state control.

---

10   For example, if residents decided upon a residents-only parking scheme – as exist in many towns in any case – homeowners without a car or who had a garage could lease their parking spaces to those homeowners who had two cars.

REFERENCES

AA (Automobile Association) (2011), 'Motoring costs 2011',
    http://www.theaa.com/motoring_advice/running_costs/
    index.html

AA (2011), *Streetwatch 3: The AA's big pothole count*, London: AA.

AIA (Asphalt Industry Alliance) (2012), *ALARM: Annual Local
    Authority Road Maintenance (ALARM) Survey 2012*, London:
    AIA.

Albert, W. (1972), *The Turnpike Road System in England 1663–1840*,
    Cambridge: Cambridge University Press.

Anderson, T. L. and D. R. Leal (2001), *Free Market
    Environmentalism*, New York: Palgrave.

Archer, C. and S. Glaister (2006), *Investing in Roads: Pricing Costs
    and New Capacity*, London: Imperial College.

Barclay, C. (2012), 'Town centres, planning and supermarkets',
    Standard note, SN/SC/1106, House of Commons Library.

Baumol, W. J., J. C. Panzar and R. D. Willig (1982), *Contestable
    Markets and the Theory of Industry Structure*, New York:
    Harcourt Brace Jovanovich.

Beckerman, W. (2003), *A Poverty of Reason*, Oakland, CA:
    Independent Institute.

Beito, D. T., P. Gordon and A. Tabarrok (eds) (2004), *The Voluntary City: Choice, Community and Civil Society*, Oakland, CA: Independent Institute.

Benson, B. (2004), 'Are roads public goods, club goods, private goods or common pools', Working paper, http://www.coss.fsu.edu/economics/sites/coss.fsu.edu.economics/files/users/bbenson/roads_public.pdf

Blankart, C. B. (2006), *Öffentliche Finanzen in der Demokratie*, Munich: Verlag Vahlen.

Block, W. (1979), 'Free market transportation: denationalizing the roads', *Journal of Libertarian Studies: An Interdisciplinary Review*, 3(2): 209–38.

Block, W. (2006), *The Privatization of Roads and Highways. Human and Economic Factors*, Lewiston, NY: Edwin Mellen Press.

Blythe, P. T. (2005), 'Congestion charging: technical options for the delivery of future UK policy', *Transportation Research Part A*, 39: 571–87.

Borcherding, T. E. (ed.) (1977), *Budgets and Bureaucrats: The Sources of Government Growth*, Durham, NC: Duke University Press.

Brittan, S. (2012), *Inside the Department of Economic Affairs: Samuel Brittan, the Diary of an 'Irregular', 1964–6*, ed. R. Middleton, Oxford: Oxford University Press.

Bryant, B. (1995), *Twyford Down: Roads, Campaigning and Environmental Law*, London: Routledge.

Buchanan, J. M. and G. Tullock (1962), *The Calculus of Consent: Logical Foundations of Constitutional Democracy*, Ann Arbor: University of Michigan Press.

Butler, E. (2011), 'Free bank shares for all is a very bad idea, Nick Clegg', http://www.guardian.co.uk/commentisfree/2011/jun/23/free-bank-shares-nick-clegg

Carnis, L. (2001), 'New directions in road privatization', Austrian Scholars Conference 7, Proceedings, 30/31 March, Auburn, AL: Ludwig von Mises Institute.

Carson, K. A. (2008), *Organization Theory: A Libertarian Perspective*, Charleston, SC: Booksurge Publishing.

Coase, R. H. (1960), 'The problem of social cost', *Journal of Law and Economics*, 3(1): 1–44.

Cordato, R. E. (2004), 'Towards an Austrian theory of environmental economics', *Quarterly Journal of Austrian Economics*, 7(1): 3–16.

Day, A. (1998), 'The case for road pricing', *Economic Affairs*, 18(4): 5–8.

Demsetz, H. (1989), *Efficiency, Competition and Policy. The Organization of Economic Activity*, vol. II, Oxford and New York: Basil Blackwell.

DETR (Department for the Environment, Transport and the Regions) (1998), *A New Deal for Transport: Better for Everyone*, London: TSO.

DfT (Department for Transport) (2004), *Feasibility Study of Road Pricing*, London: DfT.

DfT (2011a), *Reported Road Casualties in Great Britain: 2010 Annual Report*, London: Department for Transport.

DfT (2011b), *Transport Statistics Great Britain*, London: TSO.

DfT (2012a), *Department for Transport Organisation Chart 29 March 2012*, London: DfT, http://www.dft.gov.uk/publications/organisation-charts/

DfT (2012b), 'Deferred English road and rail projects', FOI response, http://www.dft.gov.uk/foi/dft-f0008526/

Dodgson, J. (2009), *Rates of Return on Public Spending on Transport*, London: RAC Foundation.

Downs, A. (1957), *An Economic Theory of Democracy*, New York: Harper.

Dudley, G. and J. Richardson (2003), *Why Does Policy Change? Lessons from British Transport Policy 1945–99*, London: Routledge.

Dunleavy, P. (1991), *Democracy, Bureaucracy and Public Choice*, London: Pearson Education.

EC (European Commission) (2003) *Information Society Technologies for Transport and Mobility: Achievements and Ongoing Projects from the Fifth Framework Programme*, Luxembourg: Office for Official Publications of the European Communities.

Eddington, R. (2006), *The Eddington Transport Study: Transport's role in sustaining the UK's productivity and competitiveness*, London: TSO.

Ellerman, D. (2001), 'Lessons from eastern Europe's voucher privatization', *Challenge*, 44(4): 14–37.

Elliot, N. (1989), *Streets Ahead*, London: Adam Smith Institute.

EU (European Union) (2010), 'Cutting road deaths by half', http://ec.europa.eu/news/transport/101012_1_en.htm

Evans, A. (1988), *No Room! No Room!*, London: Institute of Economic Affairs.

Financial Times Deutschland (2011), 'Bahn droht mit weniger ICE-Strecken', 25 April 2011, http://www.ftd.de/unternehmen/

handel-dienstleister/:konkurrenz-durch-fernbusse-bahn-droht-mit-weniger-ice-strecken/60043519.html

Francis, J. (1851), *A History of the English Railway; its social relations and revelations, 1820–1845*, vols 1 and 2, London: Longman, Brown, Green and Longmans.

Friedman, M. (2002), *Capitalism and Freedom*, Chicago, IL: University of Chicago Press.

Glaister, S. and D. J. Graham (2004), *Pricing Our Roads: Vision and Reality*, London: Institute of Economic Affairs.

Graham, D. J. and S. Glaister (2004), 'A review of road traffic demand elasticity estimates', *Transport Reviews*, 24(3): 261–76.

Harrison, F. (2006), *Wheels of Fortune*, London: Institute of Economic Affairs.

Hayek, F. A. (1944), *The Road to Serfdom*, London: Routledge & Sons.

Hayek, F. A. (1945), 'The use of knowledge in society', *American Economic Review*, 35(5): 519–30.

Hayek, F. A. (1974), 'The pretence of knowledge', Prize lecture, Nobelprize.org, http://nobelprize.org/nobel_prizes/economics/laureates/1974/hayek-lecture.html

Hibbs, J., O. Knipping, R. Merket, C. Nash, R. Roy, D. E. Tyrrall and R. Wellings (2006), *The Railways, the Market and the Government*, London: Institute of Economic Affairs.

Higgins, N., P. Robb and A. Britton (2010), 'Geographic patterns of crime', in *Crime in England and Wales 2009/10*, London: Home Office.

Highways Agency (n.d.), 'A brief history of our roads', http://www.highways.gov.uk/knowledge/1813.aspx

Highways Agency (2012), *Highways Agency Business Plan 2012–13*, London: Highways Agency.

International Road Federation (2011), *World Road Statistics 2011*, Geneva: IRF.

Kates, S. (2011), *Free Market Economics: An Introduction for the General Reader*, Cheltenham: Edward Elgar.

King, P. (2010), *Housing Policy Transformed: The right to buy and the desire to own*, Bristol: Policy Press.

Kirzner, I. (1997), *How Markets Work: Disequilibrium, Entrepreneurship and Discovery*, London: Institute of Economic Affairs.

Knipping, O. (2002), 'The Liberalisation of European Railway Markets – Laissez-faire versus Interventionism', PhD thesis, University College London.

Knipping, O. (2005), 'Running free – private ownership of roads', in J. Hibbs (ed.), *The Dangers of Bus Re-regulation and Other Perspectives on Markets in Transport*, London: Institute of Economic Affairs, pp. 94–105.

Knipping, O. (2006), 'Railway privatization in the UK – a laissez-faire approach to an interventionist failure', in J. Hibbs, O. Knipping, R. Merket, C. Nash, R. Roy, D. E. Tyrrall and R. Wellings, *The Railways, the Market and the Government*, London: Institute of Economic Affairs, pp. 159–78.

Knipping, O. (2011), 'De-nationalise our roads! Taxes on traffic would thus lack any justification', €*uro*, January, p. 22.

Landman, K. (2003), *A National Survey of Gated Communities in South Africa*, Pretoria: CSIR Building and Construction Technology.

Landman, K. and M. Schonteich (2002), 'Urban fortresses: gated communities as a reaction to crime', *African Security Review*, 11(4): 71–86.

Lomborg, B. (2001), *The Skeptical Environmentalist*, Cambridge: Cambridge University Press.

Malmberg Calvo, C. and S. Ivarsson (2006), 'Private roads to the future: the Swedish Private Road Associations', in G. Roth (ed.), *Street Smart*, Oakland, CA: Independent Institute, pp. 327–46.

MIG (Macquarie Infrastructure Group) (2006), 'M6 Toll', http://www.highways.gov.uk/aboutus/documents/MIGM6Toll.pdf

Minford, P. and J. Wang (2011), 'Public spending, taxation and economic growth – the evidence', in P. Booth (ed.), *Sharper Axes, Lower Taxes: Big Steps to a Smaller State*, London: Institute of Economic Affairs.

Mises, L. v. (1935), 'Economic calculation in the socialist commonwealth', in F. A. Hayek (ed.), *Collectivist Economic Planning*, London: George Routledge & Sons.

Mises, L. v. (1949), *Human Action: A Treatise on Economics*, London: William Hodge.

Mueller, D. C. (1996), *Public choice II. A revised edition of Public Choice*, Cambridge: Cambridge University Press.

Mulheirn, I. and D. Furness (2010), *Roads to Recovery: Reducing congestion through shared ownership*, London: Social Market Foundation.

Newbery, D. (1998), 'Fair and efficient pricing and the finance of roads', 53rd Henry Spurrier Memorial Lecture, given at the Royal Society of the Arts, 5 May.

Newman, O. (1973), *Defensible Space*, New York: Macmillan.

Newman, O. (1981), *Community of Interest*, New York: Anchor Press.

NHTSA (National Highway Traffic Safety Administration) (2011), 'Traffic fatalities in 2010 drop to lowest level in recorded history', http://www.nhtsa.gov/PR/NHTSA-05-11

Niskanen, W. A. (1971), *Bureaucracy and Representative Government*, Chicago, IL: Aldine Atherton.

Odell, M. (2012), 'Error inflated economic case for HS2', *Financial Times*, 11 April.

Olson, M. (1965), *The Logic of Collective Action: Public Goods and the Theory of Groups*, Cambridge, MA: Harvard University Press.

Parker, D. (2009a), 'PPP/PFI – solution or problem?', *Economic Affairs*, 29(1): 2–6.

Parker, D. (2009b), *The Official History of Privatisation, vol. 1: The Formative Years 1970–1987*, London: Routledge.

Pennington, M. (2002), *Liberating the Land: The Case for Private Land-use Planning*, London: Institute of Economic Affairs.

Plowden, W. (1971), *The Motor Car and Politics, 1896–1970*, London: Bodley Head.

RAC Foundation (2006), *Road User Charging*, London: RAC Foundation.

Rawcliffe, P. (1995), 'Making inroads: transport policy and the British environmental movement', *Environment*, 37(3): 16–20, 29–36.

Roth, G. (1996), *Roads in a Market Economy*, Aldershot: Ashgate.

Roth, G. (ed.) (2006), *Street Smart: Competition, Entrepreneurship and the Future of Roads*, New York and London: Transaction Publishers/Oakland, CA: Independent Institute.

Samuel, P. (2009), 'Credit Suisse say tollroad concessionaire stock prices in line with other infrastructure', *Tollroadsnews*, 17 August.

Schade, W., C. Doll, M. Maibach, M. Peter, F. Crespo, D. Carvalho, G. Caiado, M. Conti, A. Lilico and N. Afraz (2006), *COMPETE Final Report: Analysis of the contribution of transport policies to the competitiveness of the EU economy and comparison with the United States*, Karlsruhe: European Commission, DG Tren.

Schmidt, I. (1993), *Wettbewerbspolitik und Kartellrecht*, Stuttgart and New York: Gustav Fischer Verlag.

Schumpeter, J. A. (1939), *Business Cycles. A Theoretical, Historical and Statistical Analysis of the Capitalist Process*, vol.1, New York and London: McGraw-Hill.

Schumpeter, J. A. (1943), *Capitalism, Socialism and Democracy*, London: George Allen and Unwin.

Shrank, D., T. Lomax and S. Turner (2010), *Urban Mobility Report 2010*, College Station: Texas Transportation Institute.

Simon, D. (1984), 'A regional perspective on the Humber Bridge: empirical and theoretical issues', Working Paper 181, University of Leeds: Institute of Transport Studies.

Smith, A. (1776), *An Inquiry into the Nature and Causes of the Wealth of Nations*, London: Methuen & Co., http://www.econlib.org/library/Smith/smWN.html

Starkie, D. (2002), 'Road networks: efficiency, externalities and consumer choice', Beesley Lecture.

Stern, N. (2006), *Stern Review on the Economics of Climate Change*, London: HM Treasury and Cabinet Office.

Stigler, G. (1971), 'The theory of economic regulation', *Bell Journal of Economics and Management Science*, 2(1): 3–18.

Süddeutsche Zeitung (2011), 'Porsche will mit Kretschmann reden', 24 April, http://www.sueddeutsche.de/wirtschaft/

gruene-gegen-kfz-industrie-kretschmann-fordert-weniger-autos-1.1088712

TfL (Transport for London) (2007), *Central London Congestion Charging: Impacts Monitoring*, Fifth Annual Report, London: Transport for London.

Tyrrall, D. (2004), 'The UK railway privatisation: failing to succeed?', *Economic Affairs*, 24(3): 32–8.

Wellings, R. (2006a), 'Rail in a market economy', in J. Hibbs, O. Knipping, R. Merket, C. Nash, R. Roy, D. E. Tyrrall and R. Wellings, *The Railways, the Market and the Government*, London: Institute of Economic Affairs.

Wellings, R. (2006b), 'Environmentalism, public choice and the railways', in J. Hibbs, O. Knipping, R. Merket, C. Nash, R. Roy, D. E. Tyrrall and R. Wellings, *The Railways, the Market and the Government*, London: Institute of Economic Affairs.

Wellings, R. (2011), 'Comprehensive transport reform', in P. Booth (ed.), *Sharper Axes, Lower Taxes: Big Steps to a Smaller State*, London: Institute of Economic Affairs.

Wellings, R. and B. Lipson (2008), *Towards Better Transport: Funding New Infrastructure with Future Road Pricing Revenue*, London: Policy Exchange.

Williamson, O. (2008), 'Transaction cost economics: the precursors', *Economic Affairs*, 28(3): 7–14.

Withrington, P. (2004), 'Reigniting the railway conversion debate', *Economic Affairs*, 24(2): 56–9.

Wolmar, C. (2004), *The Subterranean Railway: How the London Underground was built and how it changed the city forever*, London: Atlantic Books.

ABOUT THE IEA

The Institute is a research and educational charity (No. CC 235 351), limited by guarantee. Its mission is to improve understanding of the fundamental institutions of a free society by analysing and expounding the role of markets in solving economic and social problems.

The IEA achieves its mission by:

- a high-quality publishing programme
- conferences, seminars, lectures and other events
- outreach to school and college students
- brokering media introductions and appearances

The IEA, which was established in 1955 by the late Sir Antony Fisher, is an educational charity, not a political organisation. It is independent of any political party or group and does not carry on activities intended to affect support for any political party or candidate in any election or referendum, or at any other time. It is financed by sales of publications, conference fees and voluntary donations.

In addition to its main series of publications the IEA also publishes a termly journal, *Economic Affairs*.

The IEA is aided in its work by a distinguished international Academic Advisory Council and an eminent panel of Honorary Fellows. Together with other academics, they review prospective IEA publications, their comments being passed on anonymously to authors. All IEA papers are therefore subject to the same rigorous independent refereeing process as used by leading academic journals.

IEA publications enjoy widespread classroom use and course adoptions in schools and universities. They are also sold throughout the world and often translated/reprinted.

Since 1974 the IEA has helped to create a worldwide network of 100 similar institutions in over 70 countries. They are all independent but share the IEA's mission.

Views expressed in the IEA's publications are those of the authors, not those of the Institute (which has no corporate view), its Managing Trustees, Academic Advisory Council members or senior staff.

Members of the Institute's Academic Advisory Council, Honorary Fellows, Trustees and Staff are listed on the following page.

The Institute gratefully acknowledges financial support for its publications programme and other work from a generous benefaction by the late Alec and Beryl Warren.

Other papers recently published by the IEA include:

Taxation and Red Tape
The Cost to British Business of Complying with the UK Tax System
Francis Chittenden, Hilary Foster & Brian Sloan
Research Monograph 64; ISBN 978 0 255 36612 0; £12.50

Ludwig von Mises – A Primer
Eamonn Butler
Occasional Paper 143; ISBN 978 0 255 36629 8; £7.50

Does Britain Need a Financial Regulator?
Statutory Regulation, Private Regulation and Financial Markets
Terry Arthur & Philip Booth
Hobart Paper 169; ISBN 978 0 255 36593 2; £12.50

Hayek's *The Constitution of Liberty*
An Account of Its Argument
Eugene F. Miller
Occasional Paper 144; ISBN 978 0 255 36637 3; £12.50

Fair Trade Without the Froth
A Dispassionate Economic Analysis of 'Fair Trade'
Sushil Mohan
Hobart Paper 170; ISBN 978 0 255 36645 8; £10.00

A New Understanding of Poverty
Poverty Measurement and Policy Implications
Kristian Niemietz
Research Monograph 65; ISBN 978 0 255 36638 0; £12.50

The Challenge of Immigration
A Radical Solution
Gary S. Becker
Occasional Paper 145; ISBN 978 0 255 36613 7; £7.50

Sharper Axes, Lower Taxes
Big Steps to a Smaller State
Edited by Philip Booth
Hobart Paperback 38; ISBN 978 0 255 36648 9; £12.50

Self-employment, Small Firms and Enterprise
Peter Urwin
Research Monograph 66; ISBN 978 0 255 36610 6; £12.50

Crises of Governments
The Ongoing Global Financial Crisis and Recession
Robert Barro
Occasional Paper 146; ISBN 978 0 255 36657 1; £7.50

... and the Pursuit of Happiness
Wellbeing and the Role of Government
Edited by Philip Booth
Readings 64; ISBN 978 0 255 36656 4; £12.50

Public Choice – A Primer
Eamonn Butler
Occasional Paper 147; ISBN 978 0 255 36650 2; £10.00

The Profit Motive in Education: Continuing the Revolution
Edited by James B. Stanfield
Readings 65; ISBN 978 0 255 36646 5; £12.50

Other IEA publications

Comprehensive information on other publications and the wider work
of the IEA can be found at www.iea.org.uk. To order any publication
please see below.

Personal customers

Orders from personal customers should be directed to the IEA:
Clare Rusbridge
IEA
2 Lord North Street
FREEPOST LON10168
London SW1P 3YZ
Tel: 020 7799 8907. Fax: 020 7799 2137
Email: crusbridge@iea.org.uk

Trade customers

All orders from the book trade should be directed to the IEA's
distributor:
Gazelle Book Services Ltd (IEA Orders)
FREEPOST RLYS-EAHU-YSCZ
White Cross Mills
Hightown
Lancaster LA1 4XS
Tel: 01524 68765. Fax: 01524 53232
Email: sales@gazellebooks.co.uk

IEA subscriptions

The IEA also offers a subscription service to its publications. For a single
annual payment (currently £42.00 in the UK), subscribers receive every
monograph the IEA publishes. For more information please contact:
Clare Rusbridge
Subscriptions
IEA
2 Lord North Street
FREEPOST LON10168
London SW1P 3YZ
Tel: 020 7799 8907. Fax: 020 7799 2137
Email: crusbridge@iea.org.uk